ISBN 978-1-330-27862-8
PIBN 10011113

Similar Books Are Available from
www.forgottenbooks.com

GARDENING FOR ALL.

A HANDBOOK ON
GROWING VEGETABLES AND FRUIT,

and the

PREVENTION & DESTRUCTION OF INSECT PESTS

of the Garden, and Selections of

WINDOW PLANTS & HARDY FLOWERS,

for the use of

Amateurs, Cottagers and Allotment Holders,

BY

JAMES UDALE, F.R.H.S.,

and Chief Horticultural Instructor for Worcestershire,
and Past Lecturer in Surrey and Gloucestershire ;
Author of " Chrysanthemums, their History and Cultivation."

INTRODUCTION by RT. HON. VISCOUNT COBHAM.

PRICE ONE SHILLING.

1897.

Stourbridge : MARK & MOODY, "COUNTY EXPRESS OFFICES."
London : SIMPKINS.

THE RIGHT HONOURABLE

Viscount Cobham,

(President of the Worcestershire Union of Workmen's Clubs,

which has charge of the

Gardening Instruction—under the County Council—in that County,

to whom the work

is largely indebted for wise direction and steady support),

THIS BOOK

IS

WITH KIND PERMISSION

RESPECTFULLY DEDICATED.

INTRODUCTION

I readily consented to write a few introductory words to this little volume, because I am convinced that the subject of it is one of increasing importance, and I have good reasons for knowing that the author is specially qualified to deal with it.

As long ago as 1891, the Worcestershire County Council delegated to the Worcestershire Union of Workmen's Clubs and Institutes, of which I have the honour to be President, the task of administering the portion of the Technical Education Grant set apart for instruction in horticulture. Mr. Udale was appointed Instructor, and ever since, his whole time has been devoted to giving lectures upon horticulture, visiting orchards, market, allotment, cottage, and other gardens, and giving practical advice to the cultivators on the spot.

His experience, therefore, has been exceptionally large, and few men I believe are better qualified to give wise counsel to small gardeners and fruit growers, and to prove to them what a field of profit and of pleasure is open to them, if in addition to the industry and shrewdness which they often possess they bring to the management of their land a wider knowledge of scientific principles and of the result of other men's experience. It is discouraging to note the frequent instances of slovenly or ignorant cultivation of orchards and of cottage and allotment gardens. The occupiers have forgotten the truth that in these days not even a small plot of ground can be made to pay without skilful management. The evil consequences of this mistake extend beyond themselves, for I am convinced that the future of the allotment system in the country, which has been so largely developed of late years, mainly depends upon the practical recognition of this truth by allotment holders generally.

On the other hand, there are many men, who, having proved their ability to manage small pieces of land with intelligence and profit are entitled to look forward to similar success on larger holdings, and step by step to better their position and prospects in life.

The Allotments and Small Holdings Acts were intended to promote such results, and it is much to be hoped that the ranks of the farm tenants of this country, which have been thinned by the disasters of recent years, may by their means be supplied with valuable recruits. I am sure this little work will, if properly studied and applied, prove a most useful auxiliary towards the promotion of this most beneficial object.

The book, however, is addressed to all classes of Gardeners, to the managers of many acred domains, as well as to the owners of window boxes, and attention to its precepts will increase not only the returns, but the satisfaction derived from their pursuit.

Horticulture is a delight to most right-minded persons, including many who are untrained and unscientific; but it cannot be doubted that the more knowledge there is of the mysteries and phenomena of life and growth, the more grasp of the principles upon which all progress and skilled experiment must be founded, the truer and higher will be the pleasure.

Such then is the scope and aim of this book. They are such as must commend it to all lovers of horticulture, and to all who wish to see a fresh source of profit and pleasure opened out to thousands who at present enjoy but too little of either.

COBHAM.

PREFACE

IT is not as possessing any right or power to criticise thoroughly the teaching of this book that I have acceded to its author's request that I should write a short preface to it. He is a teacher who has passed through all grades of his profession, and is an accomplished master in the great science of gardening; while I, though happy in having often been among his pupils, am still in the lower classes of the school.

But, both personally and officially, I have had many opportunities to estimate the value of the work done in Worcestershire since 1891 under the Gardening Instruction Scheme which the County Council sustain. Of this scheme Mr. Udale is the Chief Instructor, and his direction of it has been wise, sound, and abounding with good results.

It is, on every ground, a matter of deep satisfaction that there is a general increase in gardening knowledge and gardening skill. There is in Horticulture a charm which enlarges as its students advance in the understanding and practice of it. It brings delight to the beginner, and a yet deeper satisfaction to the veteran. There is delight in the first crop from one's own sowing, in the first fruit from trees of one's own grafting, in the maiden blooms from the rose which, with anxiety, labour, and some loss of blood, one first budded. But better still the delight of later years, when the man, a learner still, is also at times a teacher, when the lessons of mistakes have been acquired, and when some parts of God's varied laws of growth are better understood. Better still, because the pleasure is more intelligent and more enduring.

It is as a believer in Horticulture for profit and for pleasure that I hope greatly to find that Mr. Udale's book may have that wide circulation which will give it the large power of usefulness which I am sure that it possesses.

F. R. LAWSON.

Clent Vicarage,

CONTENTS

ILLUSTRATIONS.

CORRECTIONS.—Instead of trenches U shaped, as shown on page 12, they should be as here figured, showing drain pipe.

Scale ¼inch = 1 foot.

Apple, Early White Transparent, should appear in the list given for Culinary or Dessert, instead of in that for Culinary only.

CHAPTER I.

SOILS : Their nature and improvement.

Never before has there been such a demand for knowledge and information about gardening, and never has there been such a supply produced through the Press as at the present time. As the standard of intelligence rises, so also grow the knowledge and appreciation of the advantages of a better cultivation of the soil, to the increase of wealth, pleasure, and profit.

Occupiers of gardens are no longer content with being told what to do, how to do it and when to do it, but they wish to know *why* they ought to do certain things. This is as it ought to be. To understand why we do a thing is to take a most important step toward ensuring success for that operation ; and it is as true of gardening as of any other work. The writer, bearing the above in mind, and being desirous of supplying information in a clear form and sufficiently plain " to be understood of the people," introduces into this cheap hand-book practical facts that he hopes will be of every-day use to all gardeners.

In order to produce the best result from the soil we cultivate, it is necessary not only to dig and manure that soil, but also to know something about its nature. Without such knowledge it will be an easy matter to waste both time and money in digging and manuring ; by digging at the wrong time or in the wrong manner, and by applying the wrong kind of manure.

Soils vary in their nature (1) chemically and (2) mechanically.

(1) The chemical effects of the soil depend mainly upon certain soluble minerals contained therein, especially the Chloride of Sodium (common Salt) and Carbonate of Lime. Soda and Lime attract certain plants to which they are necessary, but they are obnoxious to others which only find refuge in soils free from them. Silica on land seems to be mainly neutral chemically. Potash is indispensable to plants, but it does not appear to exercise any appreciable influence in their geographical distribution. Magnesia and Iron enter into the composition, in a small degree, of most plants, though neither appear to exert any special influence in their geographical distribution. Nitrogen and Phosphorus are absolutely essential to vegetable life, and increase the vigour of plants grown on all soils.

As a knowledge of soils and their chemical nature is of great value to the cultivator, I here give a list of soils, with their chemical analyses, which will serve as a guide to those possessing similar soil :—

Certain marls contain

from 3·4 to 25·38 per cent. of	Alumina and Iron Oxide.
7·69 to 66·67	Carbonate of Lime.
1·82 to 2·91	Phosphoric Acid.
0·68 to 5·10	Carbonate of Magnesia.

Some clays contain

from 48·99 to 73·82 per cent. of	Silica
10·3 to 32·11	Alumina.
0·12 to 2·62	Lime.
0·91 to 3·31	Potash.
0·41 to 3·0	Magnesia.
0·44 to 2.40	Soda.
0·32 to 4·17 ,,	Iron Protoxide.

There are limestones which contain

from 44·6 to 98·40 per cent. of	Carbonate of Lime.
0·08 to 40·2	Magnesia.
1·10 to 51·4	Silica.
0·42 to 8·2	Iron and Alumina.

Different sandstones contain

from 49·4 to 98·00 per cent. of	Silica.
0·25 to 3·2	Alumina.
0·35 to 26·5	Carbonate of Lime.
0·75 to 16·1	,, Magnesia.
0·25 to 3·51	Iron Protoxide.

And some granites contain

from 44.50 to 73.70 per cent. of Silica.
     12.27 to 17.35   Alumina.
     0.50 to 9.84   ,,   Lime.
     0.21 to 3.99   ,,   Magnesia.
     2.02 to 7.24   ,,   Potash.
     2.64 to 4.21   ,,   Soda.

It will thus readily be understood how a mixed soil is so fertile, possessing, as it does, a per centage of all the chemical matter that goes to build up a plant.

A perfect soil for general cultural purposes would consist of about—

60 per cent. (by weight) of Sand.
25   ,,   Clay.
7½   Humus.
7½ ,,   Lime.

This soil would be warm, retentive of moisture, but not too retentive, contain sufficient lime and organic matter, and generally be most conducive to a healthy growth of vegetation.

(2) The mechanical nature of soils. Soils generally may be formed into eight classes, viz :—

Pure Clay (Pipe Clay).
Strongest Clay Soil (Tile Clay), 5—15 per cent. Sand.
Clay Loam,   15—30   ,,   ,,
Loamy Soil,   30—60   ,,   ,,
Sandy Soil,   60—90   ,,   ,,

The above five are supposed to contain less than 5 per cent. of lime.

Marly Soil, containing 5—20 per cent. of Lime.
Calcareous Soil, containing more than 20 per cent. of Lime,
Peaty Soil, containing 20—70 per cent. organic matter.

The three latter may be either clayey, loamy, or sandy.

The water-holding power of soils is said to be—

Clay Soil,   40 per cent. of Water.
Loam,   51   ,   ,,
Heavy Clay   61
Fine Carbonate of Lime, 85   ,,

IMPROVEMENT OF THE SOIL.

DRAINING.

All soils that are wet through being surcharged with water will be cold in proportion, and uncongenial to the healthy development of crops of fruit, vegetables, or flowers usually cultivated. Such land must be drained if success is to be achieved. The method of draining will depend upon individual circumstances, but there can be no doubt that drainage by means of properly laid drain pipes is generally the best and most durable. A good outfall is essential to success in a system of perfect drainage, but as we cannot always command such an outfall, we must do the best we can with what we have. If the outfall will permit, drain pipes should be laid thirty inches deep at the bottom of U shaped trenches ; these should be in parallel lines at distances of eighteen, twenty-four, or thirty feet apart, and running in the direction of the outfall or lowest part of the ground, where they should join a larger drain laid at an obtuse angle to the general drains, and having a good fall to the outlet.

If the above method is too expensive, the soil may be drained in a more primitive and less expensive manner. At distances of six, eight, or ten yards apart, a number of trenches are excavated. Each trench should be dug out thirty inches in depth and at least two feet wide. Throw out the top soil on one side the trench, and the soil from the bottom on the other side ; because, when the soil is again returned to the trench, we wish to keep the top soil at the top, being the best. In the bottom of these deep trenches we may place several inches of loose stones, clinkers, cinders, or refuse sticks or prunings. In the absence of any of these we may use the old stalks of cabbages, broccoli, greens, cauliflowers, &c., and a few weeds or leaves should be spread evenly over them. We ought then to shovel back the soil into the trench, first returning that which was dug from the bottom of the trench, then place a dressing of manure thereon and mix it with the soil; then return the top soil, which was first dug out, and mix a little manure with this also. The ground so treated will now be higher, warmer, and richer than the ground between the trenches; but the latter will also be improved, because the trenches will drain the land on either side. Upon the broad ridges may be sown, in due time, rows of peas and beans; and these may be followed, with advantage, by cauliflowers, cabbages, turnips, carrots, &c. Whatever kind of crop is chosen to occupy those positions, it will be found to be above the general average in quantity and quality.

OTHER METHODS OF IMPROVEMENT.

Heavy clay soil may be improved by burning or charring; but we must remember that the process of burning not only changes the mechanical nature of the soil, but also destroys the nitrogen it contains. The nitrogen must, therefore, be replaced after charring or burning by the application of manure. Charring, or burning, is also destructive of insect pests, which is a decided advantage. A thick dressing of decayed leaves or other refuse of the garden, road scrapings, lime, the finest siftings of coal ashes, will each and all materially improve such soil.

Clay loam may be treated as the foregoing, especially in regard to the application of the different kinds of materials mentioned.

Marly soils will be improved chemically and mechanically by the liberal addition of decayed leaves and weeds, road scrapings, &c.

Calcareous soil (chalk or limestone) requires plentiful supplies of manure, and decayed vegetable matter generally; and an eye should be kept to the necessity of draining.

Sandy and gravelly soils will be much improved by a judicious and periodical dressing with lime or marl, and a little burnt clay when available; also with good manurings, and liberal dressings with decayed leaves and weeds.

Peaty soils should be liberally dressed with lime, to correct their acidity ; and dressings with marl and burnt clay will increase their density and improve their retentive capacity in regard to their capacity to retain manure.

When soil is not suitable for our crops we must set about making it suitable, and not sit with folded hands complaining of our hard lot and disadvantages ; but get to work industriously, and make good use of the advantages we do possess. Plodding industry, and a wise application of knowledge, are the " open sesame " to Nature's bounteous stores.

CHAPTER II.

MANURES AND THEIR APPLICATION.

The theory of manures, and the practical application of them, is intimately connected with the knowledge of the composition of plants and of soils.

The vegetable organic constituents are composed chiefly of Carbon, Oxygen, Hydrogen, and Nitrogen. The organic compounds, denominated non-nitrogenous, are important constituents of all plants. Some of them such as cellulose, liquine, starch, gum, sugar and oily matters, are universally diffused over the vegetable kingdom.

Carbon enters largely into the composition of plants; it is said to form two-thirds of the weight of *dried* plants in general. This substance is familar to us in the form of charcoal. Charcoal is porous, and has the power of absorbing soluble gases in large quantity, and of separating saline and other matters from solutions.

Nitrogen enters into combination with Hydrogen and forms Ammonia, composed of 1 equivalent of Nitrogen and 3 of Hydrogen. Ammonia is absorbed by the soil, and may thus be rendered available for the use of plants ; clay attracting and retaining Ammonia. Part of the Nitrogen of plants is also derived from Nitric Acid and Nitrates. In order that nitrogenous matter may be formed, plants must have a supply, not only of Nitrogen, but also of Sulphur and Phosphates.

Plants are also built up of inorganic elements in conjunction with organic elements, and the chief are:—

Sulphur,	as	Sulphuric Acid.
Phosphates		Phosphoric Acid.
Silicium		Silicic Acid.
Calcium		Lime.
Magnesium		Magnesia.
Potassium		Potash.
Sodium		Soda.

Chlorine ⎫
Iodine ⎪
Flnorine ⎬ In combination with metals.
Bromine ⎭

Iron feroxide in combination with Oxygen.
Manganese,

The quantity of inorganic matter in plants is small when compared with the organic constituents ; it is nevertheless essential to the life and vigour of plants. The cell-walls cannot be formed without inorganic matters.

Silica is present in large quantity in the stems of grasses.

Phosphoric Acid is abundant in the grain of cereals, beans, potatoes, and turnips.

Lime abounds in the stems of peas, beans, clover, potatoes, cabbage, turnips, and the bark and wood of trees.

Potash, Soda, and Sulphuric Acid in peas, beans, cereals, potatoes, turnips, cabbage, beet, celery, &c.

It will thus be seen that the proper application of manures for the purpose of giving a sufficient quantity of the right kinds to plants, and with a view to true economy and profit, is a most important matter, and one requiring care and consideration. Manures of all descriptions have been condemned at some time or other, not for their own faults, but because they have been misapplied, either to the wrong crops, or at the wrong time, or in improper quantity, or to crops that required—as most do—a combination of chemicals and not one kind only. Hence the frequent and senseless condemnation, in turn, of Guano, Nitrate of Soda, Sulphate of Ammonia, Kainit, Superphosphate, &c., because one kind only has been applied to a crop that required a combination of several ; say Nitrate of Soda, Kainit and Superphosphate instead of Nitrate alone. On other pages will be found lists of certain mixtures in their proper proportions for special crops, and they will illustrate the meaning of the above remarks.

FARMYARD MANURE.

This is one of the best fertilising agents we have, when properly made and suitably preserved. It does everything an artificial or chemical manure does, and a great deal more. Farmyard manure acts both chemically and mechanically, both sustaining and increasing the depth of the soil. Its mechanical effects may be classed under five heads : First—it adds humus to the soil. Second—it makes the soil more capable of absorbing and retaining moisture. Third—it lightens the soil, and makes it more accessible to the air and easier to work. Fourth—it renders the soil darker and more retentive of the warmth of the sun. Fifth—it enables the soil to hold Ammonia and Nitrogen more readily.

The relative qualities of manures are :—

First, Fowl manure.
Second, Sheep
Third, Horse
Fourth, Pig
Fifth Cow

And their chief manurial constituents are as follows :—

One ton of	Nitrogen.	Potash.	Lime.	Phosphoric Acid.
Fowl manure contains	43 lbs.	19 lbs.	58 lbs.	39 lbs.
Sheep ,,	20 ,,	14 ,,	33 ,,	13 ,,
Horse ,,	17 ,,	13 ,,	10 ,,	9 ,
Cow ,, ,,	9 ,,	8 ,,	10 ,,	3 ,

The kind of food given to animals influences the quality of manure considerably ; that from animals fed on decorticated cotton cake being considered best, and that from rape, linseed, wheat straw, bean straw, potatoes, mangolds, swedes, and turnips in the order here given. Manure from covered yards is generally much better than that from open yards; Lord Kinnaird having produced potatoes worth £11 5s. od. from land so manured as against £7 12s. od. with open-yard manure ; 54 bushels of wheat against 42 bushels, and 215 stone of straw against 150 stone.

The manurial value of waste products may be summarised thus :—

Soot	contains from 3 to 4 per cent. of Nitrogen.	
Shoddy	5 to 8	
Dried Blood	9 to 12	
Hoofs and Horns	10 to 15	
Bones	3 to 5	,,
,,	,, 20 to 25	Phosphoric Acid.
Phosphatic Slag	15 to 20	
Carolina Superphosphate	23 to 27	,,
Wood Ashes	5 to 10	Potash.

LIQUID MANURE.

The brown liquor that frequently drains from a manure heap is the life-blood of the garden and farm. This should either be collected in wells or tanks and used as liquid manure, or it should be preserved by the proper application of litter or peat moss. When we bear in mind the fact that plants can only absorb their food in the fluid state, it follows that to allow rich liquid manure to run to waste down ditches, is a great waste of material as food for plants and a great loss of money. Liquid manure is one of the most valuable fertilising agents we have. Thousands of fruit trees of all descriptions would be more vigorous, more fruitful, and longer lived if, during winter, they were only given the valuable food that is allowed to run to waste, and for which the trees are languishing. During winter, the liquid may be applied to orchard trees in its natural state; for gooseberries, currants, raspberries, and strawberries it had better be diluted with clear water.

In spring and summer the liquid manure should be diluted with at least twice its bulk of clear water; let the maxim be " weak and often." It is also better to apply it after rain, or when the ground is generally wet. Onions, cabbages, cauliflowers, peas, beans, asparagus, radishes, lettuce, celery, rhubarb, roses, and vines are all much benefited by frequent applications of weak liquid manure, especially when growing, flowering, or fruiting freely.

EARTH CLOSET MANURE

naturally comes next to liquid manure, as being always existent where civilised human life is sustained. Its value as a manure is variously estimated. In China it has for a long period been in common use, indeed very little of any other kind is used in Chinese gardens. Dr. Voelker places a manurial value upon it at the rate of 9/- per head per annum ; Sir John Lawes estimates it at 8/10.

Dr. Voelker gives the constituents as follows :—

	Pounds per annum of all ages.
Total dry substance	45·95.
Mineral matter	10·34.
Carbon	16·85.
Nitrogen	7·94.
Phosphate	4·58.

Notwithstanding such a low valuation, it is a very stimulating manure. Its effect upon the cabbage tribe, roses, and vines is very marked, but I do not recommend its use for potatoes, carrots, &c.

Appended is a list of mixtures of chemical manures for various vegetables and fruit trees, and each mixture recommended is based upon the chemical analysis of the particular kind of plant to which it is to be applied. Each kind of plant or crop so manured will thus receive the kind of food most suitable for it, and, as a natural consequence, we shall have healthier plants and better crops in proportion as we wisely follow the most valuable information Dr. Griffiths has given. We must not do as two young farmers did a few years ago : They heard of Dr. Griffiths's recommendation of of Sulphate of Iron for beans. He does not advise much more than 1 cwt. per acre to be applied ; but they thought that quantity inadequate, and used it at the rate of 5 cwt. per acre to beans and wheat. The result was—no wheat and a damaged crop of beans ! Other people make similar errors in the application of other chemical manures, and then condemn the manure instead of their own ignorance or foolishness.

The chemical manures here recommended are intended to be used in conjunction with, or supplementary to, animal manures.

SPECIAL MANURES FOR SPECIAL CROPS.

The Manures and their proportions mentioned below are such as are recommended by Dr. Griffiths and tested by myself several years, producing better results than other combinations of the same manures tried by me and applied to similar crops growing under similar conditions.

POTATOES.

Superphosphate of Lime	7 lbs.	} per rod	5 cwt.	} per
Nitrate of Soda	3½ ,,	or	2 ,,	acre.
Kainit	3½ ,,	perch.	2 ,,	

PEAS.

Superphosphate of Lime	9 lbs.	} per rod	6 cwt.	} per
Nitrate of Soda	5 ,,	or	3½ ,,	acre.
Kainit ..	2 ,,	perch.	1½ ,,	

BEANS.

Same as for Peas, with one pound of Sulphate of Iron added per square rod or perch.

CABBAGE.

Superphosphate of Lime	2¼ lbs.		1½ cwt.	
Kainit	2¼ ,,	} per rod	1½ ,,	} per
Sulphate of Ammonia	1½ ,,	or perch.	1 ,,	acre.
Sulphate of Soda	1		½ ,,	

BRUSSELS SPROUTS.

Substantially the same as for Cabbage.

CAULIFLOWERS.

Similar to above.

ONIONS.

Nitrate of Soda	1 lb.		½ cwt.	
Guano	½	} per rod	¼ ,,	} per
Kainit	¼ ,,	or perch.	⅛ ,,	acre.
Sulphate of Iron	¼		⅛ ,,	

TURNIPS.

Superphosphate of Lime	2¼ lbs.		1½ cwt.	
Guano	2 ,,	} per rod	1 ,,	} per
Sulphate of Ammonia	¼ ,,	or perch.	⅛ ,,	acre.
Kainit ..	½ ,,		¼	

PARSNIPS.

Kainit	2¼ lbs.		1½ cwt.	
Sulphate of Ammonia	1 ,,	per rod.	¾ ,,	per acre.
Guano	2½ ,		1½ ,	

ASPARAGUS.

Kainit	5 lbs.		3 cwt.	
Nitrate of Soda	3½ ,,	per rod.	2 ,,	per acre.
Superphosphate	2½ ,,		1½ ,,	

CELERY.

Water with

Kainit	2 oz.	
Sulphate of Ammonia	1 ,,	To each gallon of water.
Superphosphate	.. 1 ,,	

LEEKS.

Kainit	1 oz.	
Superphosphate	.. 1 ,,	To each gallon of water.
Nitrate of Soda ..		

RHUBARB.

Water with 2 ozs. Superphosphate of lime	
,, ,, 2 ,, Kainit	To two gallons of water.
¼ ,, Sulphate of Iron	

TOMATOES.

Superphosphate	6 lbs.	
Sulphate of Ammonia	.. 2½ ,,	
Kainit	.. 1½ ,,	Per square rod in open ground.
Sulphate of Iron	½ ,,	

Or, Water (not over leaves) with

Superphosphate	.. 1 oz.	
Sulphate of Ammonia	.. ½ ,,	To each gallon of water.
Sulphate of Iron	. ½	

STRAWBERRIES.

Dress in spring with

Guano	.. 3 parts.
Kainit	1 ,,

Or, Water with

Guano	½ oz.	
Kainit	¼ ,,	To each gallon of water.

RASPBERRIES.

Nitrate of Soda .. ½ cwt. ⎫ Two lbs. of the mixture to
Superphosphate .. .. ¼ ,, ⎬ every 100 canes.
Kainit . ¼ , ⎭

GOOSEBERRIES.

Nitrate of Soda ½ cwt. ⎫ One lb. to three square yards.
Superphosphate .. ¼ ,, ⎬
Sulphate of Iron ¼ . ⎭

CURRANTS.---Red, White, and Black.

Same as for Gooseberries.

CHERRY.

Kainit 3 parts by weight ⎫ Three lbs. of the mixture to
Superphosphate 2 ,, ⎬ each fruit-bearing tree just
Nitrate of Soda 1 ,, ,, ⎭ before active growth begins.

APPLE.

Superphosphate
Kainit .. ⎰ Equal parts by ⎱ Three lbs. to six lbs. to each
Sulphate of Soda ⎱ weight. ⎰ tree, according to size.
   (Glauber Salts)

PEARS.

Kainit 4 parts by weight ⎫ Two lbs. to four lbs. to each tree.
Superphosphate 1 ,, ⎬
Nitrate of Soda 1 ,, ⎭

PLUMS.

Kainit 5 parts by weight ⎫ Three lbs. to six lbs. to each tree.
Superphosphate 2 ,, ⎬
Sulphate of Magnesia 1 ,, ⎭

PEACHES AND APRICOTS.

Bone Superphosphate 18 parts by weight ⎫ Three lbs. to six lbs. to each
Muriate of Potash 6 ,, ⎬ tree, according to size.
Crude Sulphate of ⎭
   Magnesia .. 1 ,, ,,

N.B.—These Manures ought *not* to be sprinkled over the leaves either
of Vegetables or Fruit Trees or Plants.

PLAN—SHOWING ROTATION OF CROPPING.

FIRST YEAR.

	2	3	4
Peas Broad Beans Runner Dwarf or Celery	Carrots Parsnips Beet Salsify	Turnips Onions Lettuce Cauliflowers Cabbage or Celery	Potatoes, Early and Late, Dressed with Chemical Manure.
Manured.	No Manure.	Manured.	No Manure.

SECOND YEAR.

2	3	4	.

THIRD YEAR.

3	4		2

FOURTH YEAR.

4	1	2	3

EXPLANATION.

The accompanying plan is intended to show how the different kinds of crops may most advantageously follow each other in four successive years, so that the same *kind* may not occupy the same ground two years in succession, and in order to economize manure and labour as well as to be most conducive in preventing various diseases and insect attacks to which the crops are liable.

The numbers in the blank spaces in the diagrams for the second, third and fourth years, are intended to indicate that on those plots the crops should be planted or sown that are under the same number in the diagram for the first year.

The rotation suggested may be altered and adapted to meet varied requirements in different gardens ; a hard and fast rule not being desirable or absolutely necessary.

CHAPTER III.

PREPARATION OF THE SOIL.

In order to obtain good fruit and vegetables in abundance, it is not only necessary to sow good seed and plant good trees of sterling varieties upon fertile soil, but that soil must be in a suitable condition for the reception of the seed and trees. In other words, the soil must be well and deeply dug, pulverised, and aerated. There are three methods of working the soil: By ploughing, digging (with spade or fork), and trenching. When the plough is used constantly upon the same ground we have shallow cultivation, and a "sole" or "pan" is formed; this "sole" or "pan" being harder and less pervious to moisture from above or below than the surrounding soil, the surplus water cannot pass freely away in time of excess of rain, neither can the moisture from below pass freely upward in time of drought; therefore, as a consequence, the roots of plants growing under such conditions will always be liable to suffer from an excess or a deficiency of moisture. Under ordinary spade culture the conditions of moisture will be more uniform and favourable to plant growth, but not so favourable as where the soil is systematically trenched. In addition, the plants have a larger larder and a larger supply of food, and the crops of flowers, fruit and vegetables will be increased correspondingly to reward the cultivator for his labour. By trenching we provide the deepest rooting medium, the largest store of food, and the most evenly moist soil for the nourishment of the crops; and by following this system of culture we obtain the highest results in quantity, quality and profit.

But each operation must be carried out with judgment and skill. The work must be done with the head as well as with the hands. Intelligent work is the best work, and the best work is the most profitable in the end. Then, if the

plough be used, plough deeply and let the sub-soiler follow
the plough to break the " pan," and the water will pass freely
downward and air will follow, thus rendering more food
available and the conditions of growth more congenial to
the crops.

· Digging must be done thoroughly. No slipshod work, if
you please! And yet, alas! How few dig properly or make
a right beginning! We see a man take the remnant of a
spade, insert it at a great slope into the soil, and just push
the soil forward with it ; he does not even turn it over! And
that man digs (save the mark!) his plot of garden ; perhaps
manages to half conceal a small quantity of manure ; plants
his trees and sows his garden seeds, and then considers
himself an unlucky man because his gardening does not turn
out a success ! Does such a gardener deserve success ? Can
he reasonably expect it ? I think not.

In order to dig properly we must make a right beginning.
We do that by digging out one spit of soil at the lowest end
of the plot to be dug—if the ground is not level—and place
the soil where we propose leaving off. There are two ways
of digging a plot of ground, one by digging right across the
plot backwards and forwards until the whole is completed ;
the other is by marking off one half the width of the plot,
digging down that, and returning up the other half and
finishing at the end near where we commenced. The latter
method has its advantages, such as saving the necessity of
moving all the soil from the opening trench to the other end
of the plot, and by rendering the task less discouraging when
we undertake a half the width of the plot at once instead of
the whole.

Having opened the first trench and placed in it any
manure or rubbish that is to be applied, take the spade—
which should be clean, and neither too large or too small—
and insert it in the soil nearly perpendicularly, drive it in to
its full depth by means of the foot, press the handle down-
wards, lift the spade and soil bodily forward, turn the spade
and soil over by a sharp turn of the wrist, and deposit the
soil in its right place in front. Most soils are improved by
being left rough when first dug, especially in autumn, winter,
and early spring, when frost and snow can act upon the
lumps of soil and pulverise them far better than man can do.

TRENCHING, OR BASTARD-TRENCHING.

By ordinary double-digging, or trenching, we bury the best soil and bring the worst soil—the sub-soil—to the top. Many cultivators who have brought the sub-soil to the top have been sorry for doing it. Twenty years ago I had a small piece of ground so done, and—I was sorry for it. Nothing prospered on that soil for several years, and it was not likely! Soil inert, deficient of plant food, was brought up and the good soil buried. Plants languished upon it, seeds and seedlings perished, decent crops were looked for in vain! Therefore I do not recommend trenching as the operation is usually performed and understood, but I prefer bastard-trenching. Bastard-trenching is a system of double-digging whereby the soil derives all the benefits of ordinary trenching and none of its disadvantages ; the good and richer top soil being kept in its original position and the poor lower soil similarly.

In commencing to bastard-trench a piece of ground, let the first and second top spits of soil be first removed (numbered 1 and 2 in the diagram), then remove the first bottom spit, numbered 3, Fig. 1, and we shall have an open trench as shown in Fig. 2.

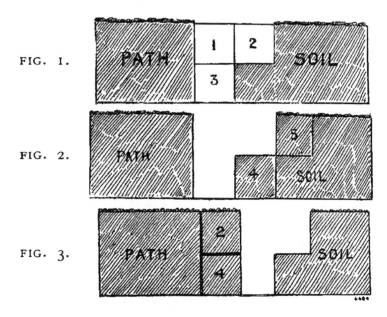

FIG. 1.

FIG. 2.

FIG. 3.

Into the bottom of this deep trench may be placed some manure or garden refuse, and, if the soil be wet, some rougher material may first be placed at the bottom to act as drainage. Then, the drainage, or manure, &c., being in, throw forward the second bottom spit of soil (No. 4 in the diagram), over the drainage, or refuse, or manure. Now add a little more manure on this lower soil that has been thrown forward, then, with the spade, take out the third top spit (No. 5), and place it over the manure and bottom soil that had just previously been moved to the front. We shall now again have a trench like the trench in Fig. 2, but, of course, the angles will not be so sharp (Fig. 3), and we proceed as before; first the drainage, rubbish, or manure, then the bottom soil moved forward, a little more manure on that, then the next spit of top soil. I trust that I have now made the operation of bastard-trenching perfectly plain to all my readers.

Another way of bastard-digging is to remove the first spit of soil, then dig or fork up the bottom soil, and at once throw on to it the next top spit of soil. It is a very imperfect method, but better to stir the bottom soil in this way than not to disturb it at all. Ground treated as previously described has yielded an increase in quantity and quality of from fifty to one hundred per cent. of vegetable crops.

BREAKING DOWN THE SOIL.

In addition to ploughing or digging the soil thoroughly, the breaking down, or pulverising it by means of the harrow or fork is of very great importance. Many persons fail to correctly estimate the value of this work. Hundreds and thousands of failures have occurred, and complaints to seedsmen have been made, from no other cause than the imperfect preparation of the soil. The seed and seedsmen have been blamed when the cultivator alone has been in fault. The quality of the materials have been found fault with when the workman deserved censure instead. Seed has been sown on hard and lumpy soil instead of upon a fine and light seed-bed.

Some has fallen into crevices, others upon stony ground, and others under clods. The moisture evaporates from the crevices and the seeds cannot germinate, or they fall too deeply in the earth. The tender seedlings cannot force their way through clods to the light, or uplift stones, and so they perish! Pulverise the soil before seed sowing! Harrow and cross-harrow it. Fork it, and fork it again, and again if necessary! This is labour well spent; it is tilling and cultivating the soil for a clear, definite, and sure purpose. For most seeds the soil cannot be worked too freely if it is at all stiff. Lighter and sandier soils are rarely worked too much, therefore break them up and give the delicate seedlings a chance to come through.

CHAPTER IV

SEEDS AND THEIR GERMINATION.

The seed of a plant is the true *fruit* of the plant, and contains within itself an entirely new plant in embryo, which, as in animal life, will resemble the parents from which it originates.

The operation of raising new plants from seed is a most interesting one to most persons, from early childhood to old age, yet the simple requirements of germination are not sufficiently understood by the majority.

Seeds vary considerably in size, from the dust-like seed of lobelia, calceolaria, and fern, to the large seed of the cocoa-nut palm and others. They also have an almost infinite number of forms, and are turned by man to as great a variety of economic uses. The seeds of Cycas circinalis are of use to the Cingalese (natives of Ceylon), in the production of bread; a flour being prepared from the seeds and made into cakes. Nutmegs are seeds of a handsome tree (Myristica fragrans), a native of the East Indian Archipelago. The seeds of the common Horse Chestnut are used in Switzerland and Turkey for feeding sheep, horses, &c. Guarana bread is made in Brazil from the pounded seeds of Paullinia sorbilis, and is sold in the form of rolls or sticks. It is used both as food and medicine, and especially in the preparation of a refreshing drink. The importance of the seed of rice, wheat, rye, lentils, peas, and beans as food for man is well known.

Some seeds or embroyos have all their nutriment contained within their own substance, especially in their cotyledons (rudimentary or " seed " leaves), and when the coats of the seed are removed, the embryo (rudimentary plant within its seed), alone is found within. Other seeds have a separate store of nutriment beside them, and when the seed coats of the embryo is found surrounded more or less completely by this nutritive matter.

The presence or absence of this nutritive matter seems to be connected with the mode in which the seed germinates, and its nature varies according as the seeds sprout rapidly or remain for a long period dormant in the soil. The store of nourishment laid up in the seed is generally greater than the embryo requires in ordinary circumstances. Some seeds continue of a soft nature, while others assume a stony hardness as in the date. Sometimes they are provided with hairy, cotton-like, and winged appendages as seen in the willow, pine, dandelion, sycamore, and cotton.

Every seed ought to be able to produce a perfect plant, but there are sterile seeds just as there are eggs incapable of producing chicks. It is important, therefore, to sow good and plump seed. A small, weak, and badly nourished seed can only produce a young plant weak in proportion ; consequently, let us be careful to save the best pods of seed from robust plants when we save seed at all.

It is best to sow new seed of peas, beans, carrots, parsnips, onions, celery, beet, and lettuce ; but new seed of cabbage, turnip, radish, cauliflower, broccoli, greens, sprouts, and kale is not so necessary, though often advisable.

GERMINATION.

Germination is the term applied to the sprouting of the embryo when placed in circumstances favourable for its growth. In the case of flowerless plants—ferns for example —a cell or spore is developed into a new organism ; while in flowering plants an embryo plant, already in a certain stage of development within the seed, begins to send forth first its root and then its cotyledons and primary stem-bud.

The essential conditions of germination are heat, water, air and darkness.   In the absence of any of these essentials there can be little or no growth.   Water is necessary for the solution of the nutritive matter of the seed and for exciting the endosmatic—or inward drawing of moisture—action of the cells.   No circulation or movement of fluids in the seed can take place until water is taken up.   Seeds imbibe a large quantity of water, and in so doing their cells become distended, by which means they are enabled to burst the hard coverings which often surround them.   Wet boots may be kept in shape and dried by filling them with oats as soon as removed from the feet ; having answered their purpose the oats may be dried and used again when required.

The amount of heat required varies very much, but generally the plants we cultivate in Great Britain, under glass and out of doors, will require warmth varying from 45° to 70° mean temperature, according to their native habitat. Heat is evolved in the process of germination.   When the seed is of good quality, containing abundance of starch, this, when the seed swells, is converted into sugary matter for its nourishment ; but if the seed is imperfect and contains gum in the place of starch, the gum is converted into vinegar and the seed decays.

Air is necessary for the purposes of germination, and the presence of Oxygen gas is required in order to aid in the changes which take place in the seed.   When seeds are buried too deeply in the soil and deprived of air, they do not grow ; but if they are brought sufficiently near the surface of the soil at some subsequent period, germination often takes place and strange plants make their appearance.

Seeds germinate more freely in darkness than in light : therefore, when small seeds like those of calceolarias, begonias, and lobelias are sown on the surface of the soil, some material such as paper, must be placed over them to intercept the rays of light.

PROPER DEPTH FOR SOWING SEEDS.

In sowing seeds, then, they must be covered with something to exclude light, the soil usually answering this purpose. They must be deep enough to obtain moisture but not so deep as to prevent air reaching them. The advantages of sowing at an even depth and at regular and proper distances are, that all the seeds germinate about the same time, and the crop arrives at maturity all at .once. Small seeds like turnip, cabbage, onion, carrot, broccoli, and sprouts may be sown about one inch deep in the soil. Smaller seeds like lettuce, endive, parsley, celery, mignonette and many flower seeds ought not to be covered with more than half an inch of soil. The smallest seeds, such as fern, lobelia, poppy, begonia, calceolaria, thyme and similar seeds are best sown upon the surface of the soil and the light kept from them by sheets of paper or other material. Larger seeds like beet-root, spinach, and lupins are best sown nearly two inches deep. Peas three inches, and beans three to four inches. All are better sown a little deeper in summer than in spring when the soil is moist.

SOWING SEEDS ON LIGHT AND HEAVY SOILS.

Light soils are generally best for the germination of all seeds and of small seeds especially, because light soil is warm, admits a sufficiency of air, contains enough moisture generally, and allows their first tender growth (plumule) a ready access to open air and light.

Heavy, clayey soil is not so suitable, because it is dense, cold, wet, and not so easily penetrated by the air ; and the seedlings cannot force their way through if sown too deeply, and such soil frequently becomes their grave.

When there is a choice of soils in the same garden, let the warmer soil be reserved for small seeds, tender and delicately rooted plants, and early crops ; the heavier soil will answer admirably for mid-season and late cabbages, cauliflowers, beans, peas, turnips, seakale, and Jerusalem artichokes ; also for winter broccoli, sprouts, savoys and curled greens.

THINNING CROPS.

All plants, whether oak trees or cabbages, require a certain amount of food and space for development. Seedling crops must be thinned timely and properly if good results are expected of them. " Sow thickly and thin quickly "

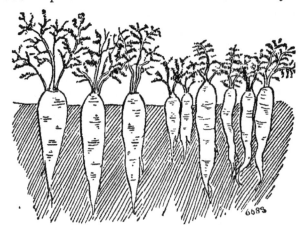

is an old garden maxim, but we must avoid sowing too thickly, which is a great evil. Onions, carrots, turnips, parsnips, beet, celery, mangolds, and all crops that are left to grow to maturity where they are sown, should be thinned as soon as they are in rough leaf, or large enough

Thinned and unthinned Carrots, showing thinned and good roots, and unthinned roots.

to easily handle. The best policy is to sow just thickly enough to secure a full crop. Overcrowding in a young state is ruinous. Too thick sowing and too late thinning has spoiled thousands of crops.

Let the gardener ever bear in mind the three essentials— Food, Air, Light—for his plants.

CHAPTER V.

THE CULTIVATION OF VEGETABLES.

DIVISION I.—ROOT CROPS.

Before proceeding to describe in detail the methods of cultivating the various crops, perhaps it will be well to give a list of varieties of the different kinds, varieties that have stood the test of many trials, under a multitude of varying circumstances, and extending over—in most cases—a long series of years. Newer varieties of proved sterling merit are introduced as being worthy of more general culture.

I now mention those belonging to the division called "root crops," other varieties will be named in the division devoted to "green crops" on another page.

As some varieties of fruit and vegetables are better, and more prolific and profitable, to grow than others, it is as cheap to grow a good thing as a bad one. A good horse consumes no more corn than a bad one, and a good variety of fruit or vegetable requires no more space or food, and gives no more trouble than an inferior variety. The culture of the best means profit, the worst frequently involves loss.

LIST OF GOOD VARIETIES OF ROOT CROPS.

Beet.—Dell's Crimson, or Black-leaved. Pragnell's Exhibition, and Nutting's Red.

Carrot.—Early Nantes, Scarlet Shorthorn, James' Scarlet Intermediate.

Jerusalem Artichoke.—New Pearly White.

Onion.—(For sowing in March) James' Keeping, Bedfordshire Champion, Brown Globe, Rousham Park, Veitch's Main Crop. (For sowing at end of July) White Italian Tripoli, Bassano Flat Red Tripoli.

Parsnip.—Hollow-crowned, Student, and Elcombe's Improved.

Potatoes.—Kidney (early)—Myatts Early Prolific, Rivers' Ash-leaved, Sharpe's Victor, Early Puritan. (Second early) —Duke of Albany, Satisfaction, White Beauty of Hebron, Webbs' Express. (Late)—Magnum Bonum, The Bruce, Reading Giant, Stourbridge Glory.

Potatoes.—Round (early)—Abundance, Early Regent, The Dean. (Main crop)—Best of All, Imperator, Paterson's Improved Victoria, Schoolmaster, and Webbs' Renown.

Radish.—Early Scarlet, French Breakfast, Ne Plus Ultra, Wood's Early Frame.

Turnip.—Early Milan Purple-top, Early Snowball, Model White Stone, Orange Jelly.

BEET.—*(Beta vulgaris).*

Beet, like similar plants, requires a deep and rich soil in which to grow to perfection. The tender and succulent roots cannot be produced to perfection in poor and dry soil ; neither will they be of the straight, tapering, and perfect form so desirable if manure is applied to them near the surface of the soil, but they will be most likely to fork and become malformed and useless.

Ground that has been liberally manured for a previous un-exhausting crop such as beans, peas, or celery, is well adapted for its requirements. In the case of following beans or peas, the soil must be deeply dug in the autumn or winter, and thrown up roughly ; this should be broken down in March and well pulverised with a fork, and again turned over several days previous to sowing the seed. If we decide to make beet a succession crop to celery there will not be any necessity to dig the ground, but simply level the celery ridges, stir the soil once or twice with the fork, and sow the seed.

Beet may be sown any time from the middle of April to the middle of May, early in late districts, late in early districts. Sow in drills an inch and a half deep and fifteen inches apart; and thin out to ten inches apart in the rows. Should there be any blank spaces in the rows they may be filled up by carefully transplanting as many as are required, taking care to remove the plants with their roots intact and keeping them well watered until they have become established.

Beet is a profitable crop to grow, and will sell for £20 to £50 per acre, according to quality, quantity, and the state of the markets; roots generally being sold retail at a penny and three-halfpence each. Beet is easily injured by frost, therefore it should be carefully lifted out of the soil in October or early in November, without breaking the root, and stored away in sand or soil in frost-proof pits, " burries," " camps," or sheds.

The root is delicious either as a pickle, or as a vegetable when baked, and deserves to be more frequently seen upon the dinner tables of the poor and middle classes; the rich have long recognised its high merit.

CARROTS.—*(Daucus carota)*.

Carrots are not one of the most certain or most profitable of crops to grow, but they answer occasionally as a break to the ordinary routine of crops on the farm and in the market garden, and they are almost a necessity in every private garden, large or small.

Their market value will vary according to the season of the year, their quality, and the general state of the crop, but it may vary from £20 to £40 per acre; a bad crop would not be worth, perhaps, more than £10 per acre, and possibly less than that amount.

Carrots do well after celery, because they delight in a comparatively light, deep, and porous soil, and old celery ground generally is rich enough in food to meet their requirements.

Sow, at any time when the soil is in a suitable condition to receive the seed, succession crops from the beginning of April to the middle of July.   Early Horn at the beginning of April, the main crop (Intermediate) about the third week in April ; and succession crops of small and juicy carrots (Early Nantes) may be obtained by sowing in June or July upon soil that has just been cleared of early peas or early potatoes.

Where very heavy soil exists there is great difficulty in obtaining a good crop of carrots.   This difficulty may be surmounted—and difficulties should only make us more determined to succeed in all we undertake—by making holes with a " dibber " at intervals of six or eight inches apart, filling them up with some light soil, and sowing three or four seeds thereon (as is often done in the case of parsnips for for exhibition purposes ; cover with the same kind of soil. Carrots generally should be sown in drills, the short rooted varieties ten inches apart and the larger kinds twelve and fourteen inches apart.   They ought to be thinned as soon as large enough to handle, from two inches to four inches apart ; this will permit of every alternate one being subsequently pulled out for use as soon as large enough, and leave room for the remainder to attain their full average size.

At the approach of winter the roots should be taken from the ground and stored away in sand, cutting off the tops close down to the root before storing them away.   I have left the roots in the soil during winter without injury, and the roots have been as sweet and juicy as when young ; but the frost in February, 1895—when the thermometer registered a temperature below zero—was too severe for them at that (my third) trial of carrots under such conditions.

Early carrots may be obtained by sowing seed on a hot bed at the end of January ; covering the manure with four inches of soil and sowing the seeds in drills four inches apart.   Also by sowing, in light soil on a warm border, at the end of February.

Dust with soot, evenly and regularly, when the carrots are well through the soil, as a preventive to injury from slugs and the carrot maggot.

JERUSALEM ARTICHOKE.—*(Helianthus tuberosus)*.

This species of sunflower, which produces the so-called "Jerusalem Artichoke," was originally introduced from the Northern United States. It has been cultivated in England as an article of food since early in the seventeenth century. The tuber does not contain starch, hence it is not floury when boiled.

Being a most wholesome and easily grown vegetable, it should be grown in every garden. It will flourish in almost any soil, and does not require much manure. It is also most accommodating as to aspect and sunshine, and will thrive in positions where many vegetables would fail.

Growing six to ten feet high, and being covered with large, bold, and artistic-looking foliage, it forms an admirable screen during summer and autumn for unsightly objects and corners in a garden.

Its stalks and foliage form also an excellent forage for cattle and rabbits, and might be more utilised for these purposes in rural and woodland districts.

Plant on deeply dug soil, in rows thirty inches apart and fifteen inches apart in the rows, and six inches deep. Planting may be done any time from the end of November to the end of March.

ONIONS.—*(Allium cepa)*.

The onion is unquestionably entitled to rank amongst the oldest of cultivated vegetables. It has a wide geographical distribution, but it is supposed to have originated in Turkestan. But of cultivated forms of the Allium, the onion does not stand alone. In addition we have the Welsh Onion (A. fistulosum), Leek (A. porrum), Potato Onion (A. aggregatum), Shallot (A. ascalonicum), Garlic (A. sativum), Chives (A. Schœnoprasum), and Tree Onion (A. proliferum).

A good crop of onions is one of the most profitable of vegetable crops, and is worth from £40 to £60 per acre ; an exceptionally fine crop in a bad season being worth much more. A good average crop would be about ten tons to the acre, these, at £4 per ton, would be worth £40. But crops at the rate of fifteen, eighteen, and twenty-two tons per acre have been produced ; these are exceptional crops.

Onions delight in deeply-worked and rich soil, and are not particular about the mechanical nature of it.

Dig the ground in autumn or winter, and apply a liberal dressing of manure at the same time.   Leave that soil in as rough state as possible in order that frost may penetrate it ; when it will be well pulverised and break down into a fine tilth at the desired time, which will be a few days before the time fixed for sowing the seed.   Before breaking down the soil with the fork, a liberal dressing of soot may be applied at the rate of three bushels per square perch ; this will, when mixed with the soil, serve both as a stimulant to the crop and a deterrent to insect pests.

Seed, for what are termed spring sown onions, ought to be sown before the middle of March.   Sow in drills ten inches or a foot apart ; cover the seed about an inch deep with soil, make the soil firm with the rake, or tread it *lightly* in if the soil is very sandy, but do not roll it or beat it down with a spade.   Thin the crop early, leaving the plants from three to six inches apart, according to the size required and the purpose for which they are grown.

When the plants are two or three inches high, let them be dusted over carefully and evenly with soot, or soot and fine lime mixed, for the purpose of repelling the onion fly when she approaches the onions for the purpose of laying the eggs from which are hatched the onion maggot.   The success of the crop will greatly depend upon the frequency and care with which this simple preventive measure is carried out.

Autumn onions may be sown during the last half of July or first week in August, and may follow early peas or early potatoes.

Scores of acres of these onions are annually sown in Worcestershire for pulling and bunching in spring, and realize from a penny to fourpence per dozen bunches.   As the seed is sown thickly for this purpose, it will be readily understood that sometimes a nice sum is obtained from half-an-acre of such onions.   Sometimes the markets are so glutted, as occurred in the spring of 1894, that it turns out to be a " losing horse," and the crop has to be ploughed or dug in.

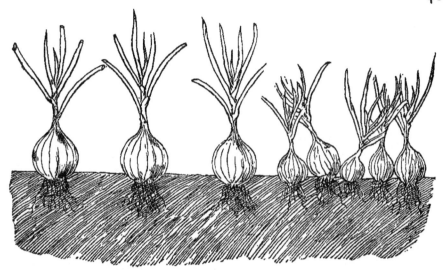

Onions, shewing the effects of thinning (on the left)
and of non-thinning (on the right).

For obtaining large onions for use the following summer,
they ought to be transplanted in March or April upon rich
soil. Let the rows be fourteen inches apart and the plants
nine inches apart in the rows. See that they do not suffer
from want of water, and feed them occasionally with weak
liquid manure ; this applies also to those sown in March.

PARSNIP.—*(Pastinaca sativa)*.

The parsnip is a native of South Europe, and takes its
name from the form of its root : **pastinum**, or dibble.

It is one of the easiest of vegetables to cultivate, is profitable to growers for market, and a delicious auxilliary to our
winter supply of food. The roots are very nutritious, and
are very valuable when potatoes are scarce, as was experienced
during the early months of the year 1895, when potatoes
rose to £6 and parsnips to nearly £4 per ton.

Sow from the middle of February to the middle of March
(but the middle of April is not too late for securing a good
crop) upon ground that has been well manured for a previous
crop, such as peas, beans, or celery, or even onions. Let the
soil be deeply stirred with the spade or fork, and when it has
settled, sow in drills fifteen inches apart. Thin out to nine
inches from plant to plant. An ounce of seed will sow a drill
eighty to a hundred feet long, and eight to ten pounds is
sufficient for an acre.

Lime is beneficial to the parsnip. Leave the roots in the ground as long as possible, and lift them as required for consumption, but a few should be lifted and stored on the approach of severe weather.

Extra fine roots may be obtained by sowing the seed upon ground that has been dug two spits deep ; also by making deep holes with a crowbar and filling up with fine and good soil, and thereon sowing several seeds, the seedlings to be reduced to one at the proper time. Some enthusiasts go to the length of using small drain pipes in which to grow their parsnips.

CHAPTER VI.

POTATOES.—*(Solanum tuberosum).*

The " homely tuber," as it is sometimes designated, is a native of Chili, and was introduced in 1596. It belongs to the Natural Order Solanaceœ, a large and widely distributed group of herbs and shrubs, most abundant between the tropics, and characterised by dangerous and narcotic properties. Familiar examples are found in the Tobacco plant, deadly Nightshade, Thorn-apple, Henbane, Tomato, Bitter-sweet, Aubergine, and Capsicum.

It was only towards the end of the eighteenth century that the great value of the potato, as a source of food, began to be realised, and its general culture for that purpose adopted. Since when it has become so important, that, in these islands of Great Britain at least, it is second only to wheat as food for the people.

" The potato is altogether the most important of root crops, not only because it is an indispensable article of food upon every dinner table, but also because it is a profitable crop when skill and judgment are exercised in its cultivation." So says Mr. John Wright in his " Horticultural Primer."

Since farmers have made it one of their staple crops, the potato has decreased in market value until the margin of profit on an average of years, is a very small one.

In Worcestershire, many thousands of acres are annually planted with potatoes, and dealers from Covent Garden visit the potato districts every autumn for the purpose of buying up the stocks. About Bewdley, Stourport, Kidderminster,

Hartlebury, Ombersley, and Stourbridge, thousands of acres
are grown, the soil being sandy, warm, and dry, and well
adapted to the cultural requirements of the potato. Good
crops are obtained, but it would be an easy matter to increase
their average by 25 per cent. if only the growers would adopt
a higher and better method of culture.

What are the conditions necessary to the healthy and
robust development of the potato plant and a good crop of
tubers ?   Deep, warm soil ; enough moisture, but not too
much ; space for the roots below the soil, and for the tops
above the soil ; a supply of proper food ; protection from
frost ; timely planting ; the planting of good, strong, and
properly prepared seed. That is the essence of successful
potato culture summed up in forty-two words.   But my
readers want details and not a summary.   Very well, I will
try to give them details, which, if they will carry into practice
intelligently, will enable them to obtain crops of potatoes at
the rate of from ten to eighteen tons per acre of late
potatoes, according to the variety of the potato and other
circumstances.

Let the ground set apart for second early or late varieties
of potatoes be bastard-trenched, as described earlier in these
pages ; this secures the deep and warm soil so desirable for
them.

No matter whether the soil be light or heavy in nature,
it should be forked over after digging, and before planting the
potatoes. If it is heavy it ought to be forked over twice.
Let the last forking be only a day or two before planting.

Do not apply fresh manure unless the soil be very sandy
or poor ; but rather plant potatoes upon ground that has
been well manured for a previous crop and which has left the
soil well supplied with nourishment.   An application of lime
at the rate of three bushels per square perch, or a dressing
with the special manure for potatoes mentioned on another
page, will be most satisfactory, and tend to a decided improve-
ment both in quantity and quality of the " noble tuber."

Plant all late varieties of potatoes by the middle of April
if circumstances will permit.   If the " sets " have been
properly stored, the young sprouts will be quite as much
advanced as is desirable or safe for them ; if they have not

been properly stored it is most probable that the young shoots will be either lost or spoiled or in great danger of being so, if planting is deferred—as I know it is by a few people—until after the period mentioned. The first sprouts are the best, therefore they should be saved if possible.

Other conditions being equal, whole sets are the best in the long run ; and those weighing 3 or 4 ozs. each, are better for producing heavy crops than are sets that are larger or smaller. I am quite aware, that, under special cultural conditions, single eyes can be made to produce heavy crops ; but, if those special conditions were withdrawn, then the single eyes would be a comparative failure, as has been demonstrated in practice.

It is better to plant in furrows rather than in holes or cups formed by a dibber. Furrows may be drawn by the plough, or the hoe, and should be three or four inches deep, according as the soil is sandy or clayey, four in sandy soil and three in stiff soil. The cups hold water about the sets, the furrows don't.

Plant widely apart, both between the rows and in the rows, in order that the plants may have space for root extension and for a free admission of sunlight to, and a circulation of air around, all their leaves and stems. A rule for our guidance in planting may be stated in this way : Plant any late variety of potato, at such distance apart between the sets in each direction, as will be nearly equal to the average height or length of the top or haulm. We do not carry this out strictly to the letter, but they who carry out the spirit of the rule reap their reward and are satisfied.

Lift the crop as soon as ripe in September or October. Select the seed at once for the following year, and, instead of placing them in heaps and covering with soil, place them (if possible) in single or double layers on shelves in light and airy sheds, or rooms, from which frost can be excluded. Then, gradually through the winter, a short, stout shoot is produced of a deep purple colour, and around its base is a mass of rootlets ready to seize and penetrate the soil in all directions as soon as planted. Growth follows with marvellous rapidity, and none of the pristine vigour of the seed has been lost.

Early potatoes may be planted fifteen inches apart in the rows and twenty-two inches between the rows when there is no intention of planting any other crop between them. Late potatoes ought to be planted in rows from twenty-two to thirty inches apart, and from eighteen to twenty-two inches from set to set in the row, according to the vigour of the variety.

RADISH.—*(Raphanus sativus)*.

The radish is a native of China, and was introduced in 1548, or forty-eight years before the potato. Many cultivated vegetables have been with us so long that it is pardonable to consider them as natives, though a mistake.

Radishes are usually a paying crop if grown tender and juicy, and early. An acquaintance of mine at Evesham, a famous market gardening district, grows nearly four acres annually.

An acre will be worth about £20, more or less; and as the crop is on the ground only about four months, from December to the end of April, the returns can scarcely be considered unsatisfactory.

The soil is richly manured for the radishes, and as soon as that crop is over, the ground is cleared, hoed, and raked, and planted in due season with vegetable marrows, ridge cucumbers, cauliflowers, or runner beans grown without sticks. These latter crops will be cleared in the autumn and the ground prepared for early spring crops of lettuce, cabbage, broad beans, or early peas, the latter to be followed in July with Tripoli onions.

The earliest radishes should be sown on warm and sheltered borders facing south. Especially should they be sheltered from the north and east winds. Sow in December if the soil is in a suitable condition to receive the seed; if it is not, sow as early as convenient in January. Rake the seed in and protect the beds with straw. This may remain on until the seed germinates, when it may be drawn off quickly, with wooden rakes, into ridges on the windward side. to ward off the cold winds, during the middle of the day, and thrown lightly over them again at evening.

A succession of tender radishes may be obtained by sowing more seed every fortnight or three weeks, according to the nature of the demand. There is practically no demand for radishes in the markets when the spring months are past. It is the early produce of all descriptions that pays the best ; late crops either yield a small profit or none, and sometimes can neither be sold or given away in the neighbourhood. Judgment and tact are required in marketing garden produce as in all other commercial pursuits.

SALSIFY.—*(Tragopogon porrifolium).*

Salsify is a British plant, and is sometimes found growing in wet meadows.

It is occasionally cultivated as a vegetable in this country, but much more extensively on the Continent.

The culture is very simple. Sow in April on ground that has been well manured for a previous crop, as for carrots and parsnips. Sow in drills fourteen inches apart, and an inch and a half deep. Thin out to six inches apart. The roots may remain in the ground, like parsnips, until required ; or may be taken up and stored away like carrots and beet.

In cooking, the roots should at first be merely washed ; then parboiled and the outside skin, which is dark in colour, be scraped off, and the roots again boiled in milk until quite tender.

SCORZONERA.—*(Scorzonera hispanica).*

Though there is a difference between this plant and salsify, the culture is similar.

TURNIP.—*(Brassica campestris, sub sp. rapa).*

The turnip is a hardy biennial found in corn fields and similar places in this country. The root, which is succulent under cultivation, is hard and woody in its wild state. Cultivation having converted it into the useful vegetable it is, neglect and improper cultural conditions soon cause it to revert to the comparatively useless nature of its wild state, hence its frequent failure in gardens.

Success in turnip culture depends mainly upon the presence in the soil of an adequate supply of food and of moisture, and an absence of insect pests, in the form of the turnip flea, the turnip fly, and slugs. A soil well supplied with lime, potash, phosphoric acid, nitrogen, and moisture, will produce good crops of turnips. Poverty and drought produces failure.

Avoid sowing turnips upon soil which has just produced a crop of cabbage, cauliflower, greens, sprouts, and the like ; but let them rather follow a crop of peas, beans, vetches, celery, or carrots.

The first sowing may be made on a warm and moist border in March. As soon as the seedlings appear, dust them slightly every evening, or as frequently as convenient, with lime, to prevent their destruction by slugs and the turnip flea.

Properly Thinned Turnips.

Successional sowings ought to be made every three or four weeks if a regular supply of tender and juicy roots is required. Thin out, as soon as the plants are sufficiently large to ensure a crop, to four, six, or eight inches apart, according to the average size of the variety and the use for which they are desired, whether for home consumption, market, or exhibition. Always remember that tender, juicy roots of medium size are always better than large, dry and woolly ones.

In July and August large sowings should be made for the purpose of providing a supply of turnips during autumn, winter and spring.

For early use sow Early Milan ; mid-season, Early Snowball and Model White Stone ; late crops, Orange Jelly, Early Snowball, and Model White Stone.

Path 30 inches wide.

Scale, ¾ inch = 12 feet.

Early Radishes, Lettuce, Potatoes, or Seed Beds.

o o o o o o o o o o o o o o o

o o o o o o o o o o o o o o

o o o o o o o o o o o o o o o

o 5 Rows Early Potatoes, 30 inches apart. o

o o o o o o o o o o o o o o o

3 Rows Dwarf Peas, 2 feet apart, without sticks.

3 Rows Dwarf Beans, 3 feet apart.

3 Rows Spring Cabbages, 2 feet apart.

3 Rows Turnips, 1 foot apart.

4 Rows Onions, 1 foot apart.

3 Rows Carrots, 1 foot apart.

2 Rows Beet-root, 18 inches apart.

3 Rows Parsnips, 18 inches apart.

1 Row Mid-season Peas.

3 Rows Late Potatoes, 30 inches apart.

1 Row Mid-season Peas, or Late Peas.

3 Rows Late Potatoes, 30 inches apart.

SOUTH. Path 30 inches wide.

NORTH. Path 30 inches wide.

Path 30 inches wide.

EAST.

Plan showing method of cropping and double or inter-cropping a small garden without fruit trees.

EXPLANATION.

The Early Potatoes are planted wider than usual in order that five rows of Brussels Sprouts o o o or Winter Greens may be planted between them immediately they are earthed up.

The three rows of Dwarf Peas such as American Wonder, William Hurst, Lightning, or William the First, should be cleared off as soon as the crop is gathered, and the ground simply hoed and raked, and at once planted with Broccoli or Savoy Cabbage for winter and spring use.

Between the Dwarf Beans or Scarlet Runners without sticks, may be planted three rows of Cauliflowers — — — for summer or autumn.

Between the three rows of Spring Cabbage are sown three rows of Broad Beans,   using the strongest seed only. If the lower Cabbage leaves are not allowed to smother the young Beans in their early stages, the Beans do well afterwards and are able to take care of themselves.

I show Late Potatoes though I do not advocate their culture in very small gardens, since they can be bought so much more cheaply than the other kinds of garden produce. Those who agree with me in this may use the ground for Celery and another row of Peas, or grow more of any kind of vegetables previously mentioned.

Cottagers with very small gardens may leave out Beet-root and Early Peas, and plant three or four more rows of Late Potatoes, keeping the same order of cropping as shown on the plan.

Where plenty of ground is at command Carrots may follow Early Peas instead of Broccoli, &c., sowing the small-rooted kinds ; they give delicious roots during autumn and winter.

CHAPTER VII.

DIVISION II.—GREEN CROPS.

ARTICHOKE.—*(Cynara Scolymus).*

This plant, commonly called Globe Artichoke, is a hardy perennial, introduced from South Europe in 1548. It is cultivated in this country as a vegetable, the part eaten being the lower fleshy portion of the imbricated scales of the parts of the flower-head termed the involucre and receptacle.

The artichoke may be propagated either from seed or by division of the plant. The latter is the method generally adopted in gardens where a stock of it exists. As it has a tendency to deteriorate in vigour after several years' cultivation, a new plantation is made every two or three years by dividing some of the older plants, and replanting in rows four or five feet apart, and three feet from plant to plant, upon deeply dug and well manured ground.

Seed ought to be sown in March on rich soil, and in rows one foot apart. Transplant the seedings, as soon as they are large enough, to their permanent quarters, the soil of which should be as advised for the divided plants. Water after planting, and during dry weather, until the artichokes are established. Hoe the soil frequently during summer and autumn. and in November place a good dressing of manure or litter close up to and around their stems to protect them from injury by frost.

By maintaining the stock of plants in a vigorous condition, a supply of good heads may be obtained from the beginning of June to the end of October.

ASPARAGUS.—*(Asparagus officinalis)*.

Although the cultivated edible species of asparagus is a native of Great Britain, yet the French have run us very closely for the championship in its culture. If the honour rested upon mere size. they would win easily ; but for size and quality combined it would be difficult to find any to surpass the best that is produced around Evesham, where there are many hundreds of acres devoted to its culture, and where it forms the chief source of revenue for the support of scores of families.

I am told that over five hundred acres were sown and planted with asparagus around Evesham, in 1894 alone ; and within a radius of six miles of that town, there are most probably, several thousands of acres planted with asparagus.

Asparagus has no rivals, in its season, amongst vegetables. Many are deterred from growing it because they labour under the popular (and erroneous) idea that it is costly and difficult to grow. That its cultivation can be made costly is beyond dispute. Two gentlemen, who attended my lectures in the autumn of 1894, informed me that they had spent five and six pounds respectively, in making one or two asparagus beds, and after waiting two or three years, had not been able to cut as many shillingsworth of asparagus. These are not isolated cases, but are fairly representative of the experience of scores of others who attempt its culture and who follow the traditional methods.

It is *not* necessary to excavate a trench four feet deep and six feet wide, and to bury therein so many scores of faggots and cartloads of manure ! Ground that is rich enough to grow a good crop of potatoes, of cauliflowers, or of onions, will grow also good crops of asparagus if given common-sense treatment in subsequent years.

We have only to sow seed, or plant one or two-year-old plants, in rows three feet apart over any area of ground, on ordinary soil, and without any further preparation than would be given for cabbage, and we may obtain as good asparagus as may be desired.

Some of the best English asparagus I have ever seen was grown in single rows eighteen feet asunder ; the ground between being occupied with the usual vegetable crops in due order of rotation year after year.

Asparagus is one of the most profitable crops to grow for market, and will realise from £30 to £60 per acre under good and intelligent management.

We may adopt either of three methods of planting asparagus, viz., in rows three feet apart over the whole area to be planted ; in narrow beds containing two rows each ; or in single rows at wide intervals of ten, twenty, or more feet apart. The two first are the best methods for growing asparagus on a large scale, and the third is well adapted for small private gardens.

Asparagus will not thrive in wet and clayey soil, nor in that which is very poor and dry ; loamy soil is best for it.

Seed may be sown in April, and, if desired, can be sown at once where the plants are to remain. In this case the seed should not be sown thickly. When the plants appear, thin them out to a foot or fifteen inches apart, but this had better be done at two operations in order to ensure a good and regular plantation. Sow the seed in drills an inch and a half deep.

When a seed bed is made by itself the seed should be sown at the usual time, and in drills a foot apart. If the seedlings are two inches apart, so much the better. The following April these plants will be in prime condition for transplanting. Choose showery weather, and lift the young plants with all their roots intact, if possible, by inserting a spade underneath them and lifting them in a body, when they can easily be separated.

Select the strongest plants for planting and reject the weaklings, because the latter will remain weakest to the end, and send up small spray instead of the desired thick and succulent heads.

Do not expose the roots longer than is absolutely necessary, because if they become dried by exposure many of the plants will die ; therefore, keep the root moist and covered from the air.

In planting, spread all the roots out around each plant just as they were before they were removed from the seed-bed ; then cover with two or three inches of fine soil. In dry weather, water should be applied until the plants are established ; where watering would be impracticable it would be best to sow seed where the plants are to remain.

The narrow beds, containing two rows of plants each, ought to be marked out three feet six inches wide, with an alley eighteen inches wide between each bed. The shallow alleys will be formed in the first instance, by simply using some of the soil therefrom for covering the roots of the transplanted seedlings, whose roots may be spread upon the surface of the bed and covered as the work proceeds. Plant at nine inches from the side of the bed, and this will leave a space of twenty-four inches between each row.

When the asparagus is established, the after culture will simply consist of periodical manuring, soiling, and cleaning.

Cover the crowns of the plants each spring with three or four inches of fine soil from the alleys or between the rows ; this should be done in February. Apply a dressing of salt in April and again at the end of June. Cut the ripe growth down at the end of October or early in November ; break down into the alleys the surplus soil that was used for covering in spring, and apply a dressing of manure. In February rake off any surplus litter that remains from the manure that was applied in November, and return the pulverised soil all over the bed, or each separate row, to the depth of four or six inches.

Additional manures for asparagus are blood, nitrate of soda, burnt seaweed, guano. and night-soil.

Under good culture asparagus will remain strong and profitable from fifteen to twenty-five years.

Many exhausted and unsatisfactory asparagus beds may be reclaimed and made more productive by allowing them a year's rest, and by exercising more prudence and self-denial when cutting, and by copious applications of weak liquid manure during the growing season as well as by stronger doses during winter. Be it remembered, that if we always cut all the strongest shoots and leave only the weak, the beds so treated must surely wear out prematurely, and we have to choose whether we will keep beds that are prematurely old through ill-treatment, and nurse them into vigour again ; or whether we will discard them and make new beds more frequently ; or whether we will treat our asparagus beds with greater kindness and forbearance from the first.

Scale, 1 in. = 16 feet.

1—10 Alleys, 2 feet wide —— — — —Asparagus.
2—10 Beds of Asparagus, 4 feet wide.
×—18 Standard Apple Trees.
✿—47 Half-standard Plum Trees.
o—150 Gooseberry Trees.

EXPLANATION.

Diagram of a fruit garden, 84ft. by 56ft., which may be extended to any size.

It is first formed into beds and alleys. The standard or half-standard apples and plums are first planted, then the gooseberries and finally the asparagus, or the latter may be sown. The asparagus and gooseberries are to pay for rent, labour and profit until the plums come into full bearing, when the asparagus may be destroyed. As the apple trees extend some of the plum trees may be removed.

Until the asparagus is fit for cutting, crops of radishes, lettuce, dwarf beans and dwarf cabbage may be taken from between the rows, and strawberries from the sides of the beds.

Currants and raspberries may, if desirable, be substituted for gooseberries, wholly or in part, and a few dwarf pears in place of plums.

———————

BEAN, French or Dwarf.—*(Phaseolus vulgaris).*

A native of the East Indies, and introduced into this country in 1597. It will not bear frost, but thrives in a high and moist temperature.

Crops of its succulent pods may be obtained the year round where a good temperature can be maintained under glass by means of hot water pipes.

For an early spring supply, sow in pots ten inches in diameter in January or February. Half fill the pots with soil containing some lime or old mortar ; place five or six seeds in each pot, and cover with two inches of soil. Water thoroughly, and maintain a mean temperature of 65°. Keep the beans near the glass, and syringe them every day to keep them clean and healthy and free from their great enemy, red spider. Make successional sowings as often as is required to supply the demand. Ne plus ultra is one of the best varieties for forcing.

Sow at the foot of a south wall or upon any other warm border, at the end of April, for the earliest out-door crop. Sow the seed two inches deep and four inches apart in the drill, and protect carefully from frost.

The middle of May is the best time for sowing the main crop, and other sowings may be made to the middle of July for the purpose of keeping up a constant supply of tender pods. Sow in drills two feet apart, or, if it is desired to inter-crop the ground, sow them three feet apart and plant a row of sprouts or cauliflowers between each row of beans.

As the tender foliage is easily destroyed by rough weather care ought to be taken to sow these beans in a sheltered position. Manure liberally for all beans.

RUNNER BEANS.—*(Phaseolus multiflorus)*.

This was introduced from South America in 1633, and is one of the most valuable and useful occupants of the kitchen garden. It is a profitable crop for the market gardener, and invaluable to the cottager.

The scarlet runner is not amenable to forcing in pots, but it readily adapts itself to various systems of out-door culture. It can be made at once most ornamental and useful. It may be trained to form lovely arcades, bowers, bushes and cones or columns ; and it is often grown as a dwarf bean, without sticks. Thousands of acres are grown on the latter method for supplying the London and provincial markets. They are sown in drills thirty inches or three feet apart, and the tops are pinched off when about two feet high. Sowing generally commences at the beginning of May, but plants raised early are liable to be destroyed by frost at the end of May and early in June. The fifteenth of May is the safest time for sowing, because the plants do not make their appearance above the soil much before June, and, therefore, are not so liable to injury.

The market gardeners of Worcestershire usually sow at the beginning of May, and in drills three feet apart. The earliest beans in the market necessarily command the best price, therefore they deliberately incur a little risk, and then attempt to make up for any possible loss by planting cauliflowers between the rows of beans, early in June. If the beans escape injury, and the cauliflowers are a success also, so much the better for the grower.

The beans are worth £15 to £25 per acre, and the cauliflowers a similar sum, or more sometimes ; and occasionally neither crop will realize the lowest of the sums mentioned. Earliness of the crop and sound judgment in marketing it are very important factors in the case.

Runner beans which have been properly staked will undoubtedly give a much larger crop than an equal number of plants grown without stakes. In gardens of small size, where room can only be spared for one row, sticks will probably be a distinct advantage. If the sticks are not obtainable, or are too expensive, the cultivator may have a good crop of beans by growing them as just described. When sticks are used they ought to be first placed in the ground and the seed sown up to them. Want of water is injurious to beans.

BEAN, Broad.—*(Faba vulgaris.)*

The broad bean is a native of Egypt, Persia, and the borders of the Caspian Sea. It is a valuable and accommodating garden crop from a consumer's point of view, but not from the grower's.

An acre will produce about one hundred and forty bushels as an average crop ; and the wholesale price varies from fourpence to two shillings per bushel. If we take the mean of the two prices quoted, we have one shilling and two-pence per bushel, which will give a total average of £8 3s. 4d. per acre ; a price that barely pays the grower for his outlay.

The most suitable soil for broad beans is a rather heavy one, containing a fair supply of lime. Those for gathering early should be sown upon soil that is a little lighter and warmer.

The earliest may be sown during the third week in October, the early Mazagan being a good variety for the purpose. Sow them in rows two feet apart and between two and three inches deep. The next batch to succeed the Mazagan may be sown in January or February, for which Beck's Green Gem is suitable. Seville long-pod and the Windsor varieties will answer admirably in March and April.

Broad beans are usually sown too thickly, and more care ought to be taken to sow only strong and clean seed. The Windsor, Seville, and similar varieties may be sown in double rows three feet apart, and the seeds ought to be not less than six inches from each other. Given space and food strong plants are the result, and vigorous plants are most capable of producing abundant crops.

Beans are a good succession crop to cabbage, cauliflower, broccoli, and kindred plants.

Broad beans are subject to the attack of the black aphis, which sometimes quickly injures or destroys the plants, as happened in 1893. On the first appearance of the aphis we ought at once to cut off the affected parts and burn them ; where this is practicable (it is scarcely practicable in whole fields of beans) and carried into effect, the attack and injury is much mitigated.

A golden rule in subduing pests and insects of all kinds is to attack them early, whilst they are few in number, and they are quickly and effectually overcome. " Delays are dangerous " in these, as in many other matters.

―――――

Varieties of vegetables are now so numerous that most people have some difficulty in making selections from the long lists of names submitted to them in seedsmen's catalogues. Not infrequently we have old friends presented to us under new names, and inferior varieties posing under dignified titles which do not belong to them.

The following list of vegetables in the division devoted to " Green Crops," is submitted to my readers in the hope that it may assist them in making choice of suitable varieties of the kinds they wish to cultivate, and as being likely to give satisfaction if cultivated under ordinarily favourable conditions :—

Artichoke.—Globe—Large Green Globe, Large Purple.

Asparagus.—Conover's Colossal, Early Purple Argentenil.

Beans.—Dwarf or French—Canadian Wonder, Fulmer's Forcing, Ne plus ultra. *Beans.*—Runner—Neal's Ne plus ultra, Painted Lady, Old Scarlet, Czar.

Beans.—Broad– Beck's Dwarf Green Gem, Green Windsor, Improved Longpod, Seville Giant.

Borecole.—Asparagus or Jerusalem Kale, Cottager's Kale, Improved Curled.

Broccoli. – Veitch's Self-protecting (November and December), Blackhouse's Winter White (January), Snow's Winter White (February). Leamington (March), Cattell's Eclipse (April), Ledsham's Latest of All (May).

Brussels Sprouts.—Aigburth, Imported, President Carnot, The Wroxton.

Cabbage.—White—Ellam's Early (spring), Early Offenham (spring), Mein's No. 1 (spring), Little Pixie (summer), Wheeler's Imperial (summer), Early Dwarf York (autumn).

Cabbage.—Red—Early Blood-red Pickling, Red Dutch.

Cabbage.—Savoy—Dwarf Green Curled, Early Dwarf Ulm, Tom Thumb.

Cauliflower.—Early Snowball (June and July), King of Cauliflowers (July and August), Walcheren (August and September), Veitch's Autumn Giant (September and October).

Celery.—Sandringham Dwarf White, Sulham Prize Pink, Leicester Red.

Endive.— Improved Green Curled, Moss Curled.

Leek.—Henry's Prize, Musselburgh, The Lyon.

Lettuce.—Cabbage– Early Paris Market, Hardy Green Hammersmith (winter), Tom Thumb. *Lettuce.*-- Cos.— Bath Black-seeded, Hick's Hardy White, London White, Paris Green, Paris White Cos.

Peas.—Early—American Wonder, Eclipse, William Hurst, William the First. Mid-Season—Duke of Albany, Autocrat, Senator, Prince of Wales, Stourbridge Marrow, Sharpe's Queen. Late—Champion of England, Ne plus ultra, Telephone, Walker's Perpetual Bearer.

Rhubarb.—Early Scarlet, Johnstone's St. Martin's, Myatt's Victoria.

Seakale.—Lily White.

Spinach —Improved Victoria Round Seeded (summer), Prickly Seeded (winter).

CHAPTER VIII.

BORECOLE, or KALE.—*(Brassica oleracea acephala)*.

This is a hardy biennial, and one of the most useful vegetables in the garden of the peer or the peasant. Its various forms will meet divergent tastes, satisfying alike the palate of the epicure and the cravings of the famished.

If an early supply of this vegetable is required, seed should be sown on a warm border about the middle of March. The main crop may be sown from the middle to the end of April. Sow in drills four inches or more apart, and cover with an inch of soil. If birds are likely to be troublesome, cover the seed-bed with a net, or, first damp the seeds and then roll them in red lead before sowing, this will make them distasteful to the birds. This simple preventive will apply to most other garden seeds for which our feathered friends may exhibit an undue partiality.

As soon as the seedlings appear above the soil, dust them once or twice weekly with fine lime or soot to prevent injury from slugs, turnip flea, and the possible deposition of eggs in their young stems by the cabbage fly. The latter did much injury in the summer of 1895 to cabbages and cauliflowers, by depositing one or more eggs in the tender stem of each plant at the surface of the soil. A maggot is hatched out of the egg, which destroys the stem just below the surface of the soil, and the plant gradually withers and dies.

As soon as the plants have two or three leaves they ought to be pricked out in rows four inches apart each way. This will induce a sturdy growth, and tend to form plants capable of developing grand heads of splendidly curled leaves and of succulent texture.

On planting out finally, choose ground in good heart, and
if it is in rich condition, do not apply any fresh manure ; but
should it be poor and exhausted, then a moderate dressing
of manure will be beneficial. Ground from which early peas
or beans are cleared will suit borecole admirably without
any further preparation than simply scuffling it and raking
off the weeds and rubbish.

Plant in rows diagonally, and two feet apart each way.

BRUSSELS SPROUTS.—*(Brassica oleracea bullata geminifera)*

The above vegetable is a deservedly popular one. It is
at once hardy, profitable, continuous in bearing, easy to grow,
delicious, and not liable to many insect attacks. It should be
given a place in every garden, whether for home consumption
or for market, because it survives and is fit for use when all
other green vegetables are destroyed by severe weather, and
are rendered useless.

An imperial acre will hold 6,970 plants at two-and-a-half
feet apart all ways. Let us suppose some are failures, and
that 6,500 good plants are left ; these, at a penny each when
full grown, will be worth £27 1s. 8d. Further, there is always
a sale for Brussels sprouts, they are rarely a drug in the
market, and they may be gathered from September to March
or April, or say, for six months out of the twelve. When
sold by weight they are usually sold by the bushel of forty
pounds, and the wholesale market price varies from half-a-
crown to five shillings per bushel, according to their quality,
the time of year, and the supply or non-supply of other green
vegetables. Can more be said on behalf of any other
vegetable crop ?

The statement has already been made that Brussels
sprouts are easy to grow. Few vegetables give less trouble.

Persons who have not the convenience of glass structures
and yet are desirous of obtaining the largest stems of sprouts
as early as possible, may sow seed about the middle of August.
The seedlings, as soon as large enough to handle, ought to
be pricked out, about four inches apart, at the end of
September. A sheltered place should be chosen for them
and some protection given them in frosty weather. **These**

may be planted out, in March or April, in rows three feet apart and thirty inches apart in the rows. The soil should be deeply dug and well manured for Brussels sprouts.

Where there is the convenience of a warm greenhouse or hot bed, as good results may be obtained from seed sown in boxes in January, pricked off into other boxes in due course, and pricked out into a cold frame afterwards ; or, they may be planted in April, direct from the boxes in which they were pricked out.

Some persons follow a not very common system of sowing the seed in March or April on the ground where the crop is to remain. Time is undoubtedly gained in this way and much labour saved ; but the ground is fully occupied from the moment the seed is sown, and there is some loss through waste seedlings, as in turnips and mangolds.

Satisfactory results are usually obtained from seed sown in a seed-bed in March, if the sprouts are required for domestic purposes only. Sow in drills, sow thinly, prick out early, plant out finally early in June if possible.

Cottagers, and those who have very small gardens, may economise their space by planting sprouts between every two rows of early potatoes. The sprouts will do well, providing they are planted before the potatoes have grown very high.

The proper time to plant the sprouts is immediately the potatoes are earthed up, then the sprouts have a chance of becoming established and of making some growth before the potatoes exhibit any tendency to overgrow them. When necessary, the tops of the potatoes may easily and quickly be placed aside by hand, without injury to the potatoes, and with much benefit to the sprouts.

. Generous treatment, thoughtful management, and close attention to simple details will ensure pleasing and profitable results.

BROCCOLI.—*(Brassica oleracea botrytis asparagoides)*.

The broccoli is a British biennial, and a perfectly hardy plant in its uncultivated state.

Many crops of broccoli are lost each winter through frost, mainly because the plants have been grown too luxuriantly and rendered less hardy than is their nature.

Inasmuch as this plant is grown for use chiefly during winter and spring, and that it must of necessity brave the cold and inclemency of our winter, we ought to adapt our cultural treatment for the purpose of producing broccoli plants that are of full size, hardy, and possessing tough woody stems ere winter sets in.

How is this hardiness to be obtained? Will it be obtained by planting upon rich and loose soil, and by crowding the plants together in some low and sheltered situation? No, certainly not! Such treatment will make them as tender as cauliflowers, and everybody is aware *they* will not stand severe frost.

We must adopt a totally different system to the one that would produce the best cauliflowers, and the whole secret and system of successful broccoli culture may be summed up in eighteen words, thus :—Plant early ; plant on rather poor soil ; plant on firm ground ; plant in exposed position ; plant widely apart.

Early planting (in June and July) gives a long period of growth and time to attain their full growth ere frost arrests all further progress.

Soil not too rich will promote toughness and fibre.

Firm soil is conducive to the formation of many fibrous roots, slow growth, short jointed and hard stems.

High positions are productive of sturdiness of character, through full exposure to wind and sun.

Wide planting ensures free access of wind and sun to all parts of the plant above the soil. And the whole produces plants most capable of withstanding with least injury the rigour of our winter. This is proved each winter in scores of cases by the plants themselves, and numbers of persons have, under my advice, demonstrated the fact—by the test of trial—to their entire satisfaction.

Seed may be sown in March or April, upon good soil. The seedlings must be pricked out four inches apart, as soon as large enough to handle, upon good soil again. Good soil is advisable in the initial stages of growth, in order to obtain strong and healthy young plants, and do not forget to dust the seed-bed early and often with soot, to prevent injury by insect pests.

When finally planting out, be sure to plant them at least thirty inches or three feet apart from each other, and where there is any danger of insect injury to stems or roots, place a little soot or lime close up to and around the collar of each plant immediately after planting.

A good additional precaution against injury from frost, is to lay all the plants with their heads to the north, in the month of November. They may be further protected in very severe weather by spreading litter or bracken among them. And persons who have pits, frames, or empty greenhouses may lift the broccoli and pack them close together with a little soil about their roots. A large number may be packed in a small space in this way, and saved from destruction, when other measures have been partly or entirely neglected.

After a very severe winter that has destroyed many broccoli and most other green stuff, a good field of broccoli would be worth from £25 to £50 per acre.

CABBAGE.—*(Brassica olevacea capitata).*

The culture of cabbage is so commonly well known that a detailed account of it will be quite superfluous, and I shall offer only a few hints thereon.

For cutting very early in spring, the seed should be sown about the sixteenth of August. An earlier sowing might be made on the seventh or eighth of the month, but the first-mentioned date is generally the safest.

Prick out, as soon as the plants are in rough leaf, three or four inches apart. Plant out into final quarters about the beginning of October. Ellam's Early should be planted in rows fifteen inches apart, and ten or twelve inches apart in the rows. Early Offenham and Mein's No. 1 are larger varieties and must have more space given them.

These early cabbages should, in spring, be frequently hoed, the hoeing will prevent the growth of weeds, admit the warmth of the sun's rays to the roots, and prevent the escape of moisture to some extent from below in dry weather. Thus the development of the crop will be materially accelerated and be ready some days earlier, a circumstance all good market gardeners are not slow to avail themselves of, making, as it will to them, a difference in the returns of, perhaps, £10 or £15 per acre.

Much growth before winter is not desirable ; but after winter is mainly gone we ought to encourage the crop to grow as fast as possible. A dressing of Nitrate of Soda in March or April will be beneficial, or Sulphate of Ammonia may be used, but either ought to be used in conjunction with Kainit and Superphosphate of Lime, as mentioned in the list of special manures for special crops on another page.

Cabbage is not much in request during summer, but in autumn there is a greater demand for it, and Early York, Enfield Market, and Cocoanut will meet all requirements. All, or any of these varieties may be sown in March or April, pricked out in May, planted in June and July, and be ready for cutting from the middle of August. After the heads of these autumn cabbage are cut, the old stems will produce delicious sprouts for use during the early part of winter if they were not originally cut too low.

Red cabbage is usually sown about the middle of August and pricked out and planted as advised for early white cabbage. Plants raised from seed sown in heat, in early spring, will produce large heads, for pickling, by the end of October.

SAVOY CABBAGE, or DUTCH CABBAGE.—*(Brassica oleracea bullata major)*.

This is a very useful vegetable for use during autumn and winter, and merits a place in all gardens.

Seed may be sown in March or April, pricked out in May, and finally planted out in June and July. Small varieties do not require much space ; eighteen inches between the rows and twelve inches in the rows will suffice. The larger kinds, such as the Drumhead, ought to be allowed two feet between the rows and eighteen inches in the rows.

These may advantageously be planted immediately after early peas, early potatoes, and early broad beans. It is unnecessary to do more than hoe and rake the weeds and rubbish off after either of the above crops are cleared ; the labour of digging may be avoided, and the savoys will prosper.

Either of the three kinds of cabbage mentioned, are usually a profitable crop to grow for market ; but much depends upon the season, the distance from market, the market itself, and the number and wealth of the population ; and, above all, the earliness or otherwise of the crop.

An acre of cabbage in the middle of April may be worth £30, a fortnight later it may not be worth more than £10.

CAULIFLOWER.—*(Brassica oleracea botrytis)*.

The cauliflower is the most delicate variety of the cabbage tribe. It was first brought into England from Cyprus, and it was cultivated, though as a rarity, in the beginning of the seventeenth century.

By the end of the following century its cultivation had become so common and extensive that English cauliflowers were exported into Holland, Germany, and France.

It requires a richer soil than, and as much space as cabbage ; and as a much smaller portion of the plant is used as food, it can never become so cheap an esculent.

The best crops are obtained by planting upon well manured and deeply-dug soil. It will not bear our English winter, therefore, on the approach of frost, protection must be afforded.

For the production of the earliest crops, seed may be sown from the fifteenth to the twenty-fifth of August. The seedlings should be pricked out, either into cold frames, or on a sheltered and warm border. These require much attention during the winter months, in the matter of protection from frost, and destruction by slugs, mice, and rats ; and from decay through excessive moisture. Constant care must be given in regard to ventilation, and also to make firm the plants as often as they become loosened or thrown out of the soil by the action of worms. It will thus be seen that these autumn sown cauliflowers are a never-failing source of trouble and anxiety, from the end of October until the middle of the following June, when we may reasonably hope to be secure from frost, and commence to cut some cauliflowers as a reward for our labour.

Where there is a heated greenhouse at command there will not be much necessity for sowing the seed of early cauliflowers in autumn. In fact, if the seed is sown in boxes in the month of January and kept near the glass in a greenhouse from which frost is always excluded by means of fire-heat ; and if the seedlings are pricked out into other boxes and receive ordinary care, there will be very little difference in time of cutting between those sown in January and those sown in August.

I find, on reference to my diary, that I have cut cauliflowers on June 20th from seed sown in the autumn, or about ten months after sowing. They were sown on August 3rd and planted out on March 29th. Seeds of Early Snowball, sown in boxes on February 13th, 1883, gave heads on June 28th, or a little more than four months after sowing. The same variety, sown February 12th, 1884, were ready for cutting on July 9th, and the same results were obtained in other years by the same variety, and from Early Erfurt and Veitch's Early Forcing. It is thus clearly proved, that by sowing early under glass, cauliflowers can be, and have been grown in about half the time of those sown in August ; and there is a difference of only a few days in the time of cutting ; a difference that could easily be removed at the first attempt, if desired.

Seed of any variety, except Autumn Giant, may be sown in the open border in March and April, and they will give a supply during August, September and October.

Autumn Giant is a grand and useful variety, but, owing to its immense size, it requires a long period of growth— about five months from the time of planting. It should be sown in a frame or a box in February, and the seedlings pricked out and grown on liberally until large enough to plant out. Plant them thirty inches apart ; other varieties will answer well two feet apart ; and Snowball, Erfurt, and similar varieties may be planted a little closer together.

Manure liberally for cauliflowers, and grow them as fast and luxuriantly as possible. Never forget that throughout the season of growth, crops make incessant demands upon the soil for their sustenance.

A PLAN for Planting and Cropping a small Garden or Allotment with Fruit and Vegetables. The end border nearest the house may be planted with flowers, the border farthest away with Rhubarb or raising Seedling Plants. The outh may be used for Salading, or more Strawberries or Flowers. If the Asparagus is not required the ground may be used for more of any of the vegetables paid.

PATH.

PATH.

PATH.

PATH.

N
W E
S

Scale, 1 inch = 20 feet.

A a A
B b c B
C d e C
D f g h i j k D
E l m n E

EXPLANATION.

A.A. Standard Apple Trees.

B.B. Pyramidal Pea s.

C.C.   ,,   Apples.

D.D.   ,,   Plums.

E.E. Standard Damson and Plum.

✱ Red Currants.

× Gooseberries.

• Strawberries.

a. Raspberries, 3 rows.

b. Row of Scarlet Runners.

c. Late Potatoes, 9 rows.

d. Early   ,,   6 ows, 3 feet apart.

Brussels Sprouts to be planted between.

e. Broccoli, 5 rows.

f. Peas, 3 rows. ▐█▌▐▌█▐▌

g. Cabbage, 3 rows.

h. Cauliflower, 2 rows.

i. Turnips.

j. Onions.

k. Carrots.

l. Parsnips, 2 rows.

m. Broad Beans, 2 rows.

n. Asparagus, 3 single rows.

CHAPTER IX.

CELERY.—*(Apium graveolens)*.

The celery plant belongs to the natural Order Umbelliferæ, growing wild in many of the southern parts of Europe, and is not uncommon in the Isle of Thanet and other marshy spots of England near the sea.

It has been greatly changed and improved by cultivation, and now presents numerous varieties, some of which are used for salad, while others, including what is called the turnip-rooted sort, are much used for stewing or similar purposes. In soups the seeds may be used equally with the stems or leaves.

A light rich and rather moist soil is best adapted for its growth, whilst one that is heavy, wet, and adhesive, is unfavourable to it. Although the plant requires plenty of water during its growing period, yet it is apt to rot in winter, especially upon cold, heavy soils. Provided abundance of manure can be supplied, a poor light soil is better than one that is stiff and rich ; for the growth can be made to depend chiefly on the manure supplied, and the plant grows better when its leaf-stalks are surrounded with light porous soil than when it is pressed against by hard and heavy soil when earthing-up has commenced.

The largest celery is usually grown in single or double rows in trenches, six or eight feet apart, as at Sale, near Manchester ; but the system of bed-culture, as practised at Tamworth, produces more heads from the same space of ground. In the latter system the beds are marked off four, six, eight, or ten feet wide, and as many yards long as the ground admits of. Five or six inches only of the top soil is removed to either side of the bed for use in earthing-up ; a heavy dressing of manure is given and carefully forked in, and the celery planted nine inches apart in straight lines *across* the bed.

Boards, nine inches wide and the exact width of the bed, are used to facilitate the earthing-up operation. One board is placed against a row of celery, and a second board against the next row of celery, each board facing the other. Soil may then be thrown between the boards without damage to the plants, and the usual process of placing it around each plant with the hand goes on with ease.

The routine of cultivation is very simple, and two requirements must always be complied with if success is to be attained, viz. :—An adequate supply of moisture and of food must always be present from the time the seed is sown until growth is completed.

For early crops, sow seed during January in shallow pans or boxes of light soil, and place the same in a warm and light greenhouse or hot-bed until the seedlings have made three or four leaves ; when they must be transplanted into a frame or into other boxes, using a good rich compost of loam, leaf-mould, and well-rotted manure incorporated thoroughly together. Keep them growing until the end of May and then plant out in trenches in the usual way. Very early celery may be obtained by leaving plants eight inches apart on the hot-bed, where they will grow vigorously, and blanch them by tying brown paper round each plant.

For later crops, sow in heat in February and in a cold frame in March, treating the young plants as before advised. Plant out in June and July, lifting the plants as carefully as possible with a good ball of soil, and plant them in the well-manured beds or trenches nine inches apart; a good watering will then complete the operation. Do not earth up too early, or apply too much soil at one operation.

ENDIVE.—*(Cichorium Endivia)*.

Although endive has become a common garden plant, it is not really hardy. It was introduced from India in 1548, is easily grown, and is most useful for household purposes in winter.

It is known under two forms, the curled and the Batavian, both forming well-known salads by the blanching of their leaves. The curled has beautifully crimped and curled leaves, which are tender and much esteemed ; the Batavian has leaves which are nearly flat, and being more hardy, is so much used that it forms the principal winter salad.

The first sowing may be made about the second week in June, and subsequent sowings in July and August. Sow the seed on rich soil, and when large enough, transplant into rows a foot apart and about nine or ten inches apart in the rows.

When fully grown each plant should be tied up, the outer leaves being tied together over the inner leaves, that it may be blanched. Or blanching may be done by placing a tile or slate over each plant, or by inverting a flower-pot over each plant and covering the hole to exclude the light. On the approach of winter the endive may be lifted with a ball of soil and planted in a dark shed or dry cellar, from whence it can be used as required.

LEEK.—*(Allium porrum)*.

Introduced from Switzerland in 1562, the leek has long been a favourite esculent, and its culture becomes more extended each year.

During the winter of 1894-5 it proved itself almost invaluable, because it was one of only three kinds of vegetables which withstood the extreme severity of the weather with very little injury.

Its cultivation is very simple. Sow in February and March, on light and rich soil, in drills four or five inches apart. Encourage a robust growth by thinning the seedlings to two inches apart. Plant out on rich ground, in beds, nine to twelve inches apart in the rows, or in well-manured trenches as for celery, if the largest leeks are desired. Plant in May and in June.

Prior to transplanting the plants from the seed bed, they ought to receive a thorough watering and then be loosened with a fork, in order that their roots may be easily and safely withdrawn from the soil. Use a trowel for planting in trenches, and a dibber for planting in beds.

The after culture is the same as for producing good celery. Give abundance of liquid manure.

LETTUCE.—*(Lactuca sativa)*.

The lettuce is a smooth, herbaceous, annual plant, containing a milky juice, which has been cultivated from remote antiquity, and is in general use as a salad. The original locality is unknown. The immature plant only is eaten, as it is narcotic and poisonous when in flower. Over twenty species of Lactuca are known from various parts of the globe. The inspissated or thickened juice, known as lettuce-opium, is used medicinally to allay pain and induce sleep.

Lettuces form a profitable crop to grow if obtained and sent to market early in the season. The tenderest and most appreciated lettuce is that grown in borders, early in spring, under glass. The seed may be sown in autumn, planted in the borders in November, and the crop sent to market in February. Seed sown in January will produce plants ready for sale in April if grown under the same conditions as the previous.

Many acres are grown about Evesham and sent to market early in the spring. These are obtained from seed sown in September and October and planted out under shelter of the fruit trees and fences, at the end of October and beginning of November, where they receive much protection from frost.

Large quantities of excellent lettuces are grown under bell-glasses and hand-lights, and come into use a little earlier than those under the trees, &c.

A pinch of seed of Tom Thumb or Early Paris Market sown in a box in February, and planted out in April on a warm and sheltered border, will give good and crisp lettuce at the end of May and early in June.

A later and successional supply will be obtained by sowing in the open border in April, and at intervals up to, and including, August. Vacant spaces between celery trenches may be utilised with advantage by planting them with lettuce, and not infrequently the best lettuce is produced there.

Cold frames are useful in which to shelter lettuce during winter ; and in cases where the plants are frozen, it is best to gently thaw them by sprinkling cold water over them, and by sheltering them from the rays of the sun until completely thawed.

Those plants intended to pass through the winter ought to receive abundance of room, air, and light at all times, except when there is frost. Good lettuce can only be produced on rich and moist soil in conjunction with a warm temperature.

Some good gardeners grow a hardy variety under the name of "Schofield" ; it withstands an ordinary winter tolerably well, and comes early into use in spring.

PEA. – *(Pisum sativum)*.

The pea is a deservedly popular occupant of the kitchen garden, and the cultivator who succeeds in annually producing good crops of peas of the best quality performs a feat of which he may be justly proud.

There are many varieties of peas in cultivation, and many more have passed out of cultivation and are forgotten, and deservedly so.

In the Gardeners' Year Book for 1873 we find 79 varieties figured, most of which have ceased to exist, but a few were varieties of sterling merit and they are with us to-day ; amongst which are Sangster's No. 1, William the First, Laxton's Supreme, British Queen, Ne plus ultra, Champion of England, and Veitch's Perfection. On page 71 of that useful book we find these opening sentences :—" During these twenty years the numerous names that have been given to the different varieties of peas have been most puzzling, and have led to great confusion. A variety of great excellence is allowed to degenerate, and in due course it gradually becomes like anything but what it originally was. Some grower has been careful to keep his stock very select, and finding in time that it is much superior to the degenerated one which is in general cultivation, he concludes that he has secured something new, and presently announces it to the world under a new name, and at a high price. But it is the old variety notwithstanding."

The foregoing remarks are so true of fruit, flowers, and vegetables generally that I offer no apology for quoting them.

Peas do well upon stiff and calcareous soil ; but when sown upon light soil they must be abundantly manured. They require a good supply of potash, lime, magnesia, soda, and phosphoric acid, and a constant supply of moisture ; drought is nearly fatal to peas. In fact, food and moisture in abundance are absolutely necessary for the production of good crops of peas.

The earliest crops of peas are obtained by sowing seed at the end of October and early in November on a warm border, in rows three or four feet apart ; these usually produce pods for picking early in May. As there is some risk of injury to these early sown peas on account of their having to withstand the inclemency of winter, and a greater liability to the depredations of mice and birds, they are seldom sown except in large private gardens. Peas may be obtained earlier by sowing on borders under glass frames, or in large greenhouses.

January and February is usually soon enough for sowing early peas, and these will produce pods ready for use early in June, and sometimes at the end of May if they have been well sheltered and protected. Sow in rows four feet apart in warm and sheltered positions.

Successional sowings may be made up to June, which will keep up a supply as long as the weather will permit the plants to continue active circulation of the sap. Sow in rows twelve feet apart, and plant other vegetables between the rows.

The mid-season and late crops ought to be sown in rows twelve to twenty feet apart in gardens, the plants then will be healthier and stronger for not being overcrowded, and will produce enormous crops of splendid peas, and the ground between the rows will produce good crops of other vegetables.

Care should be taken to avoid sowing peas too thickly in the rows, especially in regard to those that grow three feet high and upwards. Many crops of peas have been ruined mainly because they have been sown too thickly, this tells especially during periods of drought and in cases of insufficient manuring. All rows of peas should run north and south. Manure liberally for them at all times.

Peas are a profitable crop to grow for market and will realise from £10 to £30 per acre. Usually those grown in fields vary from £10 to £20 per acre on the ground. These are generally sown in February and are cleared off the ground at the end of June and early in July, and are succeeded by a crop of swedes or cabbage.

RHUBARB.—*(Rheum hybridum)*.

This commonly grown and handsome looking plant was introduced from Asia in 1778. It is one of the most useful crops for home use and a very profitable one when properly grown and marketed.

As a market crop it is most profitable when lifted and forced and sent to market from December to March, after which time the price falls very low. The sum realised may be anywhere between £20 and £60 per acre, according to circumstances.

Seed may be sown upon an ordinary seed bed in March. Sow in drills one foot apart, and thin out the young plants to nine inches apart. These should be planted in due time in their permanent quarters, the ground having been previously deeply dug and heavily manured, planting in rows four feet apart and the plants three feet from each other in the rows.

Old roots may be divided and re-planted, the roots being divided by a sharp spade with as little injury as possible, taking care that each root has a strong crown attached. Each root is then planted in rows four feet apart and three feet apart in the row.

Rhubarb is easily forced by lifting the roots and packing them closely together in a dark and warm shed, filling up the spaces with soil and keeping the roots moist. Or by covering the roots in the ground with boxes or barrels and heaping warm litter over all. A mean temperature of 60°

suits rhubarb admirably. It may be forced a little in a cellar, and a mushroom house at work is a most admirable place for forcing it.

SEAKALE.—*(Crambe maritima)*.

Seakale is a hardy perennial, growing naturally on the coasts of England and Scotland, as well as France and the shores of the Baltic.

The people on the western shores of England have, from time immemorial, been in the practice of watching when the shoots begin to push up the sand or gravel in March and April, then cutting off the young shoots while still blanched and tender, and boiling them for food.

When cultivated in gardens the young shoots are blanched by being grown in a dark shed, cellar, or mushroom house ; or by covering with pots or boxes ; or by drawing soil over the crowns.

Unfortunately this plant is only cultivated in large private gardens and in market gardens, but it merits a wider culture, especially by amateurs. Its culture is extremely simple although it requires to be blanched ; and seakale pots are unnecessary.

It requires rich and well-manured soil, and very strong plants may be grown from root-cuttings or " whips " in one year ; indeed, I never grow seakale more than one year, and therefore raise a new stock of plants every year from root-cuttings.

Where root cuttings are not available a stock of plants may easily be raised from seed. Sow the seed in March or April where it is to remain. Sow in drills twenty-two inches apart and thin out the plants, when they appear above the soil, to twelve or fifteen inches apart. These seedlings may be allowed to grow a second year, at the end of which they will be very strong and suitable either for forcing, or for blanching and cutting where they stand.

Culture from root cuttings consists in selecting clean, straight cuttings, about five inches long and half-an-inch or five-eighths of an inch across, from the older roots, either during winter when roots are lifted for forcing, or from the old plants as they are dug up to be thrown away after their heads are cut in March and April from the open ground.

As these cuttings are taken from the parent plants, the lower portion should be cut slanting, and the top should be cut square across, this is for the purpose of readily distinguishing the top from the bottom after they have been laid aside. These may be tied in bundles and buried several inches deep in sand, soil, or ashes, keeping the crown end uppermost, and just exposing these to air and light.

In April these cuttings must be planted on rich soil, and at distances apart to be regulated by the system of culture adopted. If to be lifted for forcing during the winter, then they may be planted in rows twenty or twenty-two inches apart ; but if the roots are to grow and the crop to be cut direct from the ground, then the rows must be thirty inches apart.

Plant the cuttings with a dibber and cover with nearly an inch of soil, having previously removed all but two or three young shoots to each crown. When the plants are established and growing, remove all the shoots but one upon each plant, and the one left ought to be the strongest and best.

If the weather is dry at the time of planting, water must be applied freely until the plants are established. The after culture will consist of hoeing freely to keep down weeds and to encourage rapid growth. Salt is a good manure for seakale and may be used at the rate of ten or twelve hundredweight per acre.

Roots may be lifted for forcing as soon as the foliage has decayed in November if required. Plant the roots thus lifted, in dark sheds, mushroom-house, or boxes, and let the roots be from four to six inches apart ; give a good watering, and in a month or six weeks—according to the temperature —the seakale will be ready for cutting. In February and March it may be had in a fortnight or three weeks after planting in the mushroom house.

The out-door culture simply consists of digging a trench or furrow between each row of seakale before it commences to grow, and placing the soil over each crown, and thus form a continuous ridge about nine inches high over the seakale. Excellent blanched seakale is thus obtained, and it is cut as soon as the tips begin to show through the soil, this being cleared away at the time of cutting.

Seakale is a profitable crop to grow, realising prices varying from fourpence to eighteen-pence per pound.

SPINACH.—*(Spinacea oleracea).*

The culture of spinach is so simple as to require little explanation. It is usually sown between rows of early peas, but there can be no doubt that it succeeds much better where it obtains more air and light.

A supply is easily maintained by sowing at intervals from the beginning of February until September. The crop to stand the winter must be sown in a dry position, at the end of August and another sowing in September; the two sowings are advisable because, sometimes, the first sowing is too forward to survive the winter.

Sow in drills fifteen inches apart, and that intended to survive the winter ought to be thinned out to fully six inches apart in the rows. Protect from slugs with ashes, sawdust, soot, or lime.

CHAPTER X.

MISCELLANEOUS CROPS.

CUCUMBER.—*(Cucumis sativus)*.

The common cucumber is supposed to have been originally imported into Europe from the Levant as early as 1573. Cucumis Melo is the common melon, supposed to be a native of Persia. Water melons are the fruits of Citrullus vulgaris, commonly cultivated in the east, and Mediterranean region of Africa and Europe, for the sake of its fleshy edible fruit.

Cucumbers are easily grown either on ridges, in frames, or in hot-houses. Ridge cucumbers are a very profitable crop; Mr. F. Eccles, of Wyre, near Pershore, informs me that he has realised as much as £90 per acre for them, and he puts their average value at £45 per acre in ordinarily favourable years. A variety called " Stockwood " is one of the best for ridge culture. For this system the seed may be sown in small pots, at the end of April, in a warm frame or hot-bed, placing three or four seeds in each pot, and leaving only the two best plants that are produced. At the end of May the ridges or mounds (the latter is the method adopted in Worcestershire), may be prepared by simply excavating the soil about a foot deep, and placing in the hole or trench some warm manure. A hole two feet across is usually sufficient in a warm and sheltered district; in less favoured localities larger holes or broader trenches must be made, to hold more manure for the purpose of supplying more warmth to the roots.

Place six inches of soil over the manure, using the soil that was excavated if it is of good and suitable quality, and plant the cucumbers. Protect with hand-lights and keep them raised slightly from the soil. Water carefully, as required, until the plants are thoroughly established.

Where there is not the convenience of a frame or hot-house for raising the plants, seed may be sown direct upon the mounds or ridges, but in this case they ought to be prepared at the beginning of May instead of towards the end of the month.

Frame cucumbers or hot-house cucumbers may be sown in any month of the year, according to the time the fruit is required and the means at command for growing it. Those who depend upon frames for a supply, may sow in March or April, in three-inch pots, three parts filled with good soil. Plunge the pots in a hot-bed, or bottom heat of some kind. At this early stage be careful only to apply water of the same temperature as that in which the plants are growing, and any soil placed in contact with the plants should be previously warmed.

In about a month they will be ready for planting into the frame where they are to fruit, the soil then for them should be composed of leaf mould, rough loam, and decayed manure in equal parts. Make up the hot-bed a few days before planting out, and, after planting, shade for several days, until the young plants are established.

The temperature for the frame at night should be 65° to 70°, and in the daytime it may vary from 80° to 95°

Cucumbers are lovers of atmospheric moisture, and they dislike cold currents of air at all times. When the sun is very bright and hot the cucumbers ought to be shaded with thin material of some kind, or whitewash the glass.

With proper attention to heat, careful watering—avoid giving too much,—stopping at one or two joints beyond the fruit, and an occasional cutting out of old and barren growths, plants in frames will bear from May to the end of September.

Fifty fruits from each square yard of space occupied by cucumber plants is a nice crop. Rollisson's Telegraph is one of the best for frame or hot-house culture.

VEGETABLE MARROW.—*(Cucurbita esculenta)*.

This is a very popular vegetable, easy of culture, and as much at home in the back garden of the peasant as in, the extensive kitchen garden of the nobleman.

If trained up substanital trellis-work, it is most ornamental and striking, and is only then seen in its most beautiful and interesting aspect, especially when bearing some of its handsome as well as useful fruit.

Its good culture is so similar to that described for ridge cucumbers, that the *modus operandi* need not be repeated. In addition, the plant will succeed on heaps of garden refuse over which a few inches of soil has been thrown, on exhausted hot-beds, or in warm positions on richly manured ground.

Gourds and pumpkins prosper under the same conditions, and are most ornamental objects either in growing or when the fruits are grouped together on shelves. tables, and in recesses in winter.

Good crops of vegetable marrows bring to the grower £20 to £30 per acre, but it must be remembered that it is mainly the early fruits which make such an average possible, mid-season and late vegetables are often un-remunerative.

TOMATO.—*(Lycopersicum esculentum)*.

Tomatoes are the fruits of a South American plant, which plant is closely allied to our common potato, and is attacked by similar diseases—species of fungi, one kind attacking the root and stem, and producing the " sleepy disease," a second, the leaves, and a third, the fruit. The first is called *Fusarium lycopersici*, and the first indication that a plant is diseased is shown by the drooping of the leaves, which increases day by day. As a rule the plants are attacked when quite young, but the outward evidence of the disease does not manifest itself until the plant is full grown, or even not before the fruit is set. Plants manifesting the above symptoms should be at once carefully removed—roots and all—and burnt, and the soil be promptly dressed with quicklime, mixing the two thoroughly.

The leaves are attacked by a fungus called *Cladosporium fulvum*, which manifests itself by spots upon the leaves, and in time destroys the whole of the leaves affected.   On the first appearance of this disease, the affected parts ought to be sponged with a solution of sulphide of potassium, at the rate of half-an-ounce of sulphide to one gallon of water, and an occasional spraying with the same mixture will hold the disease in check.   A cold and damp atmosphere pre-disposes the plants to this disease, and if there is an excess of moisture at the roots, and imperfect ventilation in addition, the disease is most likely to be very serious in form and extent.   A free circulation of air, a warm—but not hot—temperature, abundance of light, proper food, and enough—but not too much—water, will secure healthy and very fruitful plants if the variety is a good one.

The fruit is liable to be attacked by the black spot fungus, *Cladosporium lycopersici*.   It is liable to attack all varieties, and under any system of cultivation.   Spraying with a weak solution of sulphide of potassium may be of service as a preventive, but all fruits attacked must be removed and burned as soon as they are noticed, because the disease is in the interior of the fruit and beyond the reach of direct applications of fungicide.

Tomatoes have become so popular that tons of the wholesome and medicinal fruit are grown and consumed now, whereas twenty-five and thirty-five years ago only a few pounds were required.

All persons who have "a bit of glass" wish to grow tomatoes, and even those who have no glass wish to grow a few.

The culture of tomatoes is very simple and easy.   Sow seed in January, February, March, or April, according to the time the fruit is required and whether to be grown under glass or in the open air.   For the latter purpose the beginning of April is early enough to sow the seed if artificial heat is at command.

Drain, and nearly fill with good soil, some six inch pots. Press the soil down very lightly and evenly, and sow the seeds one inch apart all over the surface of the soil, cover with three-quarters of an inch of soil, water the seed nicely, and place in frame, green-house, or hot-house, according to circumstances. Thin sowing produces sturdy plants, thick sowing produces weak and spindling ones.

When large enough to handle, transfer the seedlings into small pots—one plant in each—filled with light and rich soil. As they advance in size and vigour give them another shift into four-inch or six-inch pots, using a similar soil to the above, and grow on in such a position as will afford warmth, light and air, and keep them near the glass.

Harden them off gradually in preparation for planting out of doors, and they may be planted out finally at the beginning of June, the second week in June being usually safer from frosts than the first week. Obtain the plants in flower at the time of planting if possible, and if a bunch of fruit is already set, so much the better. Trim off all superfluous side-shoots, and, if grown in the open ground, take off the top of each plant when five or six bunches of fruit are set. Those grown against walls may be allowed to grow a little higher, because they will possibly ripen a few more fruits.

Do not cut or mutilate any of the principal leaves if room can be found for them ; this applies to plants growing under all circumstances, either out-of-doors or under glass.

The details of culture under glass are similar to those already described, especially if grown in pots, with this addition, that when the pots are filled with roots and the plants are carrying a crop of fruit, it will be almost impossible to over-water (if the drainage is right) or overfeed them.

I prefer to plant tomatoes in borders under glass ; to plant them two feet from each other all ways ; to train each plant vertically towards the glass, and to confine each plant to one stem.

Where space is plentiful and the supply of plants limited, then more than one main stem may be taken from each plant ; in fact, as many as are required to fill the space at command. Half-a-hundredweight of tomatoes have been gathered from one plant grown in this way. These main stems should be trained about eighteen inches apart.

The best varieties are :—Early Chemin, Laxton's Open
Air, Sutton's Earliest of All, Orangefield Dwarf, Greengage,
Ham Green Favourite, Hackwood Park, Dedham Favourite,
Carter's Early Ruby, Early Evesham, and one raised by
Mr. Gilman at Alton Towers.

MUSHROOM.—*(Agaricus campestris)*.

The common mushroom, so well known in this country,
is considered among the most savoury of the genus, and is in
much request for the table.   The St. George's mushroom
(A. Georgii), and the Fairy-ring mushroom (A. Oreades), are
also edible.

Mushrooms are cultivated in sheds or houses specially
constructed for them, and in other sheds and out-houses ; on
ridges in the open air ; on hot-beds, and in fields.

" Though belonging to a low order of vegetation (says
Mr. J. Wright), mushrooms contain more nitrogenous matter,
and in that respect more nearly approach animal food than
does any other vegetable."

Few things grown out of doors are so profitable as full
crops of mushrooms.   Mushrooms can easily be grown during
autumn, winter, and spring in any ordinary shed, cellar, or
out-house where the temperature does not fall below 45°, and
is tolerably uniform.   Having had considerable success in
mushroom culture, I will briefly describe my method.

Collect the fresh horse-droppings from the stable every
morning.   Do not have any from other but well and hard-fed
horses ; never use that from horses fed on grass or other
green food.   Separate only the long litter from the droppings,
and allow the short to remain mixed with them.

Spread the manure about nine inches thick over a floor
in any shed from which rain is excluded.   When sufficient
material is collected to make a bed of the required size, throw
the whole into a heap to ferment.   In two or three days the
manure will be quite warm, if not hot, it should then be
thoroughly turned over to allow the foul gases to escape.
After another day or two the material will either be in a
suitable condition to at once be made into a bed, or it will
require another turning, each heap of manure has to be dealt
with on its merits, but usually it is ready after the first or
second turning.

The best site for the bed is a hard dry floor, in any of the before-mentioned structures, or a similar site in a sheltered position out of doors, if the ridge system is to be adopted. The best moderate size for a bed is one, six feet by four, but almost any size may be made, the size only being limited by the supply of material at command. An uniform depth of twelve inches is very favourable for flat beds, and ridges ought to be about thirty inches high and three feet broad at the base when it is intended to make beds in that way, whether under shelter or out of doors.

Commence to form the beds by forming a layer of manure about eighteen inches thick, tread or beat this down quite firmly, then add more manure and treat it in the same way until the requisite depth has been obtained. A stick should then be inserted in the bed to test its temperature. When the heat has fallen to 85° or 90° it may be spawned with safety.

Spawning requires more care than is usually bestowed upon it. A dibber should not be used, because that makes a round hole which the piece of cake containing the spawn seldom fills, steam or vapour generates around the sides, and the spawn perishes before it can penetrate the manure in which it is intended to grow.

The spawn should be inserted by raising a little of the manure with the hand and placing the spawn underneath, pressing the manure down again firmly, but not covering the spawn more than half-an-inch deep. Each piece of spawn should be two inches square, and be inserted from four to six inches apart.

Soiling or " casing " may be done as soon as the spawn is inserted. Moderately strong loam should be used if obtainable, if not, use the next heaviest. Apply sufficient to leave the soil one inch in depth after it has been beaten down with the spade or other tool used for the purpose. Make it quite firm and smooth, and for this purpose the soil must be moist at the time of application. Dry soil cannot be rendered firm and smooth.

Cover the bed with hay or litter after soiling; the depth of covering having to vary with the surroundings of each case, whether in the open air, in dry and draughty sheds, or moist and close mushroom house. The greater the liability to atmospheric changes the thicker must be the covering of protective material. Do all that is possible to keep the bed in an atmosphere that is uniformly warm, moist, and dark.

Gather the mushrooms carefully, and be sure to remove the entire stem along with the mushroom, because, when cut off, the portion of the stalk that is left decays, and that decay passes on to the spawn which would otherwise have remained sound and productive. Should the bed become very dry water it very carefully with warm water.

For a continuous supply, a fair-sized bed should be made every month, commencing at the end of August. A cart-load of manure will make a bed about five feet square ; or a ridge thirty inches high, thirty inches broad at the base, and nearly five feet long.

Given attention to the details here plainly set forth, there is no reason why all who can obtain suitable manure should not grow mushrooms for their own use and to increase a possibly scanty income.

HERBS.

Just as a coat is incomplete when minus one sleeve, so is a kitchen garden incomplete without its row of parsley and herb bed.

New potatoes and green peas are better for just a suspicion of mint about them, broad beans for their parsley sauce, and the duck and onions incomplete without the sage.

PARSLEY—*(Petroselinum sativum)*

is most easy to grow, but not often seen in the best condition.

Sow seed in rich soil in March for summer and autumn use, and at the beginning of July for use in winter. Thin out the seedlings freely to five inches apart at the first thinning, and afterwards remove every other plant. If more parsley is wanted, the thinnings may be transplanted carefully. Under these conditions fine and beautifully moss-curled parsley may be obtained year after year. Parsley is usually very inferior through being over-crowded.

MINT—*(Mentha viridis)*

may easily be propagated in spring, by taking young shoots with a small portion of root attached, and planting in a shady position until established, or by affording protection with a hand-glass ; and by ordinary division of the roots.

SAGE—*(Salvia officinalis)*

is easily raised from seed ; or from cuttings, four or five inches long (taken off with a " heel " like a rose cutting) taken in June and inserted in sandy soil in a shady position under a hand-light ; also by layers, as every old housewife knows full well.

PENNYROYAL—*(Mentha pulegium)*

may be rooted from cuttings in spring or autumn ; or raised from seed. All herbs may be raised from seed as easily as celery, and under the same system in the early stages of growth.

THYME—*(Thymus vulgaris)*

can easily be obtained from seed, thousands of seedlings sometimes springing up about old plants; also by cuttings and layers.

SWEET MARJORAM—*(Origanum marjorana)*

is raised from seed ; or from cuttings struck under a hand-light, or in a cold frame in June.

SWEET BASIL—*(Ocymum basilicum)*

being a tender plant, should be sown in boxes or pots, and transplanted in open ground at the beginning of June; after which several sowings may be made each month up to September.

Borage, Buglas, Chervil, Coriander, Clary, Summer Savory and Purslane are all best propagated by seed.

Balm *(Melissa officinalis)*, Tarragon *(Artemesia dracunculus)*, and Chamomile *(Anthemis nobilis)* may each be easily propagated from seeds, cuttings, or by division of the roots.

CHAPTER XI.

HARDY FRUITS AND THEIR CULTURE.

SMALL FRUITS.

The culture of fruit in these islands has received a great impetus during the past ten years. Never has there been a higher or more correct value placed upon good and wholesome fruit, as a source of food, than at the present time; and never has it been offered to the public in such great abundance or of such high quality. Yet the full value of such fruit is not appreciated by all. Many regard it as a luxury only to be enjoyed on special occasions, and spend more money upon other and more doubtful sources of food and refreshment than is at all necessary. To others, unfortunately, it is yet a real luxury difficult to obtain. Let us hope the time is not far distant when the poorest may be able to purchase an abundant supply of really good fruit at a reasonable price. At present I know—from weekly and sometimes daily observation of the markets, and daily contact with the growers—that the consumer seldom pays less than one hundred per cent. more for garden produce than the producer receives. For example; yesterday, August the first, 1896, I saw some Rivers Early Prolific Plums offered at fourpence per pound; that would be at the rate of one pound six and eightpence per bushel of eighty pounds, for which the grower would receive ten or twelve shillings per bushel. Also English apples were offered at threepence per pound, or at the rate of sixteen shillings per bushel of sixty-four pounds, while the growers of those apples were receiving five and six shillings per bushel; a difference of two hundred per cent!

The same is true of vegetables. In the year 1894 I saw beautiful Autumn Giant cauliflowers offered in the streets at twopence and threepence each, the growers were receiving three farthings each for them. During the summer of 1896 a dealer bought vegetables of me, took them straight to the consumers and charged double what I charged him. He got his money, but I still wait for payment,—January 4th 1897. And so the robbery of the producer and consumer continues year after year. I do not suggest how this comes about, I only state the facts, and indicate the great blot which stains the fruit and vegetable commerce of this country.

The remedy for such a state of things, is to do all that is possible to bring the producer and consumer into closer contact with each other, to their great mutual advantage.

Allotments are doing much to mitigate the evil of a scarcity of vegetables and fruit among the poor in rural districts, and to a lesser degree near large centres of population, but hundreds of thousands remain at the mercy of dealers and middlemen.

At no previous time has such a general desire shown itself for improving the condition of artizans and labourers as the present, and for developing the resources of the soil by the production of an adequate supply of home grown fruit.

Fruit culture, well and wisely conducted, may be, and is a source of profit to many ; and a good supply of sound and ripe fruit is a great benefit to the general community. But care must be taken not to be misled by foolish statements seen in print of immense sums per acre being realised for certain kinds of fruit. I do not say that those statements are inaccurate, but I do say that they are misleading, inasmuch as they represent very exceptional cases and are far removed from *average* prices, which, after all, form the only sound basis upon which to make safe calculations.

We have orchards in great numbers, but their occupants, in far too many cases, are trees that were planted generations ago and are now too old, or are very inferior varieties. These ought to be superseded by young trees of the best varieties, carefully selected, and planted in good positions. And, in addition, we ought to pay more attention to the art of placing the fruit before the public in the most attractive and honest manner, by separating the superior from the inferior fruit, and by arranging that the fruit at the top shall be a fair sample of the whole of each package.

CURRANTS.—*(Ribes rubrum & nigrum)*.

There are three kinds of currants in general cultivation —red, white and black. As the cultural details of red and white currants are the same, I shall deal with the two as one —red. The black currant is of a wholly different habit and must be managed differently.

Red currants, like to all fruit trees, may be raised from seed, but they are usually raised from cuttings. The shoots selected for cuttings should be firm, straight, clean, short-jointed, as thick as a lead pencil, and about fifteen inches long when the top has been cut off.

Prepare the cutting by making a clean cut at the base straight across and just below a joint. Carefully remove, with the point of a knife, all the buds from the base and lower part of the cutting, leaving only four or five at the top. If the buds have been properly removed, this will ensure a clear stem of several inches above the ground, a thing most desirable in red currants and gooseberries.

The cuttings should then be planted in straight lines fifteen inches apart, and six inches apart in the lines. Plant the cuttings firmly and deeply, leaving several inches of clear wood between the soil and the lowest bud.

At the end of the first year each rooted plant should be transplanted, either to where it is to remain permanently or into nursery lines ; and, if they have made good growth, the shoots may be pruned to half their length, cutting to a bud that points in the direction in which the branch ought to grow, which is usually *outwards* and *upwards*.

Red currants are amenable to various styles of training, but they usually produce the best results from bushes. Trees trained grid-iron form upon walls produce abundance of fruit of the finest quality. Fruit so grown is easily protected by netting from the depredations of birds, and it will hang until after Christmas in fresh condition (and exceedingly luscious) if the aspect is either north-west, north, or north-east. Frequently have I had red currant tart to dinner on Christmas Day, the fruit having been gathered direct from the trees !

Shoot of Red Currant, summer-pruned at **A, B,** and **C.**

A well-shaped currant bush will have seven to nine branches. These will be of nearly equal strength and length, and will radiate from the main stem at about six inches from the soil, and equal distances apart from each other. The side shoots will not be allowed to become of undue length, but will be cut back to within half-an-inch or an inch of the main branch, to form compact fruit-spurs, as shown. This severe pruning will be carried out each winter, and the operation will be as rapid as it is simple.

Summer - pruning is of great benefit to currants. This is a very simple process also, and merely consists of cutting the side shoots back to three or four leaves at the beginning of July, which admits the summer wind and sun with their fructifying influences, converting useless and sappy wood into fruitful wood, *(See figure of summer-pruned shoot)*. When the trees are managed in this way in regard to summer and winter pruning, and kept well nourished, the branches are annually clothed in dense masses of fruit.

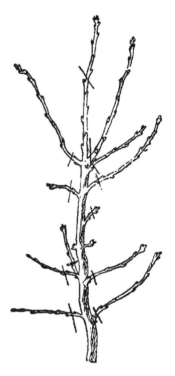

A branch of a Red Currant Tree unpruned. The cross-bars indicate the places where the side-shoots should be cut off.

Few plants are more easily managed than red or white currants, and the former yield an average of about £40 per acre under good management.

BLACK CURRANTS.

The black currant is a general favourite, and we are not likely to suffer from an over-production of it at present.

Really good crops have brought to their owner as much as £90 per acre, but these crops are above the average ; £60 is the average value per acre. Plentiful as they have been some years, they have sold at one and tenpence per dozen pounds on the ground. If we allow that a full grown bush will yield on an average 15 lbs. of fruit, and we have 889 trees to the acre at seven feet apart, we have at once a value of over £101 per acre at the above price. This high average is seldom realised.

Cuttings similar to those advised for red currants should be chosen, but it is unadvisable to remove any of the lower buds, because in this case, we wish to encourage the production of young growth from below the soil; black currants bearing most freely upon well-matured wood of the previous year's growth.

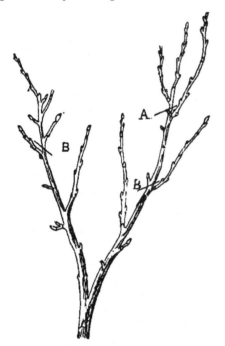

A branch of a Black Currant tree. The cross-bars at A and B B indicate the parts to be removed, according to circumstances, sometimes at A and B, and in other cases at B B.

The secret of success then, in the culture of black currants, being the annual production of young wood and the removal of the old and exhausted wood, it is obvious that proper pruning will entirely consist of judiciously making room for the young by *thinning out* the old. Leave the young shoots four or five inches apart; and new branches from below the soil are to be encouraged so far as there is space for them, because they are renewing the tree constantly.

A spade ought not to be used among fruit trees in ordinary routine work, but the annual applications of manure will be more beneficial if left upon the surface of the soil, because the manure assists in retaining the moisture about the roots as well as supplying the requisite food. If the manure on the surface is offensive to the eye, it may be carefully pricked in with a fork without breaking or tearing the roots.

An occasional dressing of lime is beneficial to currants, and it is said common salt is good for black currants, at the rate of one ounce to the square yard.

GOOSEBERRIES.—*(Ribes Grossularia)*.

Gooseberry trees are easily propagated from cuttings, like currant trees. Choose straight, firm shoots about fifteen inches long, and as thick as a slate pencil. Shorten the top a little, remove all but four or five buds, and also the spines from the lower part of the cutting.

Plant the cuttings firmly in lines or rows, as recommended for currants, and give them the same treatment during the first year. At the end of the second year the young trees will be ready for planting into their permanent positions.

Gooseberry trees are seldom grown in other than bush form, but they are both ornamental and fruitful when grown to wires—espalier or grid-iron form—alongside walks and paths ; and trees so trained have two distinctly practical advantages, viz., the fruit is easily gathered, and the trees are more easily pruned.

Pruning gooseberry trees is seldom a pleasant employment, but there are right and wrong methods of doing this as in doing everything else. The task is much easier when commenced and carried through in the right way. The wrong method is frequently the most difficult of execution and the most harmful to the tree and its owner, and his pocket.

If all the young shoots of a healthy and vigorous tree are persistently pruned to a half or a third their length, that tree will sooner or later be either a thicket of useless and barren wood, or fruitless through sheer decrepitude.

The right method of procedure in pruning a gooseberry tree is, first to entirely remove any branch that is too near the ground ; then to remove the shoots or branches that cross each other, and those that are overcrowding the tree. In cutting out these branches, care ought to be exercised to make smooth cuts in order that they may heal up quickly, and not allow water to lodge upon the surface of the wounds. Also, no "snags" should be left, but the cut be made close up to the branch from which the misplaced one is being removed.

Shoot of Gooseberry, summer-pruned at **A**, **B**, **C**, and **D**.

It will now be found that the trees do not look so formidable, that the task of pruning is reduced in dimensions and difficulty, and that little more remains to be done That " little " simply consists of thinning-out the young shoots to four or five inches apart cutting the shoots off at half-an-inch or an inch from their base to form fruit-spurs. Any remaining young shoots that are less than six inches long need not be touched ; those over six inches and less than a foot long may have a third of their length removed ; those shoots over a foot in length may be shortened nearly one-half. This kind of pruning practically ensures crops of fruit every year, and the fruit is gathered with little trouble and injury.

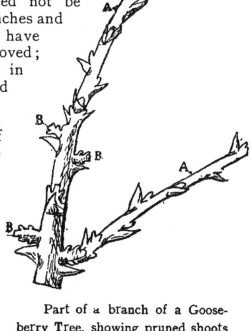

Summer pruning may be practised with great advantage upon gooseberry trees ; the work is done at a time of year when it may be carried out with comfort, the trees are directly benefited, and it saves much work in winter.

Part of a branch of a Gooseberry Tree, showing pruned shoots at **A A**, and spurs left at **B B B**.

RASPBERRY.—*(Rubus Idæus).*

Raspberries are a favourite fruit, and among the easiest to cultivate. They are also very profitable when well grown, which is not always the case. Too often they are cultivated in such a manner as to reduce their fruit-bearing capacity and to shorten their lives. The customary practice is to leave all the young growths to crowd and smother each other until the following winter, when all old and superfluous canes are cut out, and the remainder shortened to some fancied and particular height.

Manure is then applied and dug in with the spade, masses of roots are cut off in the operation each year, and the plants become weaker each successive season until they are almost worthless.   That is how *not* to grow them.

The raspberry delights in a deep, fertile, and moist soil, but it cannot withstand stagnant water.   It is usually found growing, in a state of nature, in cool and moist woods where the shade is not dense but where they obtain some sunshine during the day. Consequently, the raspberry is a very valuable plant to culti-vate as an under crop, particularly under plum trees ; but, of course, it is most profitable when grown in open and sunny positions.

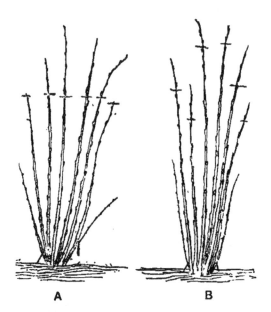

A   B

A shows the old style of pruning Raspberries, B shows the new and better style of pruning.

In preparing for a new plantation of raspberries, the ground should be deeply dug, or trenched, and heavily manured. This will permit the strong " anchor-roots " to penetrate deeply, and they will also be provided with abundance of food.

When selecting canes for planting—which may be done from November to March—choose medium-sized and well-ripened canes rather than large and gross ones ; the former will produce the best canes for subsequent fruiting.   Let these be cut down to eight or nine inches from the soil, in order that their whole energy may be directed into forming good new canes for subsequent fruiting, instead of being wasted in producing weak and useless side-shoots on the greater part of the unshortened cane.

Many are tempted to plant very strong canes with the hope of obtaining both fruit and good new canes the first year after planting; in this they are nearly certain to be disappointed, because such canes rarely develope fruit or canes of any use the first year, so a year is lost.

The most productive method or style of planting raspberries is in continuous lines, the canes being tied to wires or laths; this style is the best for gardens, especially small ones. In fields and market gardens they are usually planted in single "stools" at three feet apart—with or without stakes—and four feet from row to row.

The early summer management of raspberries consists of pulling up all weak and superflouous young growths, leaving four or five of the strongest to each stool, and in keeping the ground clear of weeds. If mulching was not put on before, to conserve the moisture about the roots, it ought to be applied now.

In autumn the old canes that have fruited should be cut out—the beginning of September is a good time—and their removal will allow a free access of light and air to the canes that are to produce fruit the following year, giving them greater maturity and fruitfulness.

If the previous cultural details have been attended to there will not be much work to do about the raspberries in winter. What remains to be done will mainly consist of tying in the canes where support is given; shortening them a little—but not too much; hoeing and raking the ground about them and applying the usual dressing of manure; spreading it on the top of the soil as far as the roots extend around, and *leaving it there*. In case of heavy soil the surface may be pricked over with a fork, avoiding going down to the roots · but light soil is better left alone, except with the hoe.

STRAWBERRY.—*(Fragaria vesca)*.

Strawberries constitute one of the most profitable crops of the garden or allotment. It is the favourite fruit of all classes and is rarely produced in too great abundance.

The strawberry-plant comes into bearing sooner than any other fruit, producing, under good cultivation, a paying crop in twelve months after planting.

The nail-makers of Catshill, near Bromsgrove, have long found the strawberry a source of benefit even upon their hungry, sandy, and dry soil, and many acres are entirely planted with it in their allotment fields. In consequence of the depressed state of the nail-making trade and of prevailing low prices—in fact, semi-starvation wages—the allotments have been found a great boon, and altogether, they now have three or four hundred acres in the district, a great portion of which is cropped with strawberries. If the crop is profitable on such poor soil, it would be, and is, much more profitable on good soil.

Good average crops of strawberries from gardens or allotments are worth about £40 per acre : those under ordinary field culture about £30 ; heavy crops of extra fine fruit would realize higher values, especially if ripe a few days earlier than the average.

July and August are good months for planting straw-berries, and these may follow early peas or early potatoes. Strawberries planted at this time will produce fair crops the following year if they have been well cared for, and if a few spring-sown onions, radishes, lettuce, or dwarf cabbage are taken from between each row of strawberries, they will pay for rent and labour and leave the crop of strawberries for clear profit, thus saving a year and all expenses. Straw-berries may also be planted in April, or during autumn and winter.

In preparing for planting, rows should be marked out thirty inches apart ; small holes should be scooped out, and if available, some manure water poured in ; this will both supply the plants with moisture if the soil is dry, and afford food in an immediately available form.

Plant the strawberries twenty or twenty-four inches apart in the rows, and be careful not to plant the crowns either too deeply or too high.

Young plants produce the strongest runners, and young plants not bearing fruit produce the earliest runners. The best general policy is to take runners from the youngest fruit-bearing plants, then there is likely to be the smallest possible percentage of barren plants in the new plantation.

When the young plants are established they will commence to send out new runners, but these must be assiduously cut or pinched off, and the whole energy of each plant be directed into developing and perfecting plump and strong crowns and good foliage.

The after culture will consist of the usual routine of mulching the plants each winter with long manure—or manure containing plenty of litter or straw—having previously hoed and raked off the weeds, and broken the surface of the soil an inch or two deep with a fork. This mulching supplies the requisite food to the plants, prevents the escape of moisture from the soil in times of drought during spring and summer, and the washed litter assists in keeping the fruit clean, thus easily "Killing three birds with one stone." In addition, the preservation of moisture about the roots of the plants, during the flowering of the plants and the " swelling " period of the fruit, materially increases the quantity and size of the fruit. Cut off all runners as fast as they appear (unless they are wanted for propagating purposes), and destroy all weeds immediately they are seen.

By following the foregoing simple process of culture, all persons with available ground (which is not a bog) may grow for themselves good crops of this delicious fruit.

LIST OF

THE BEST VARIETIES OF SMALL FRUITS

most suitable for general purposes.

CURRANTS.

Black.—Carter's Champion, Lee's Prolific, Black Naples, Baldwin's.

Red.—Grape, Raby Castle, New Dutch.

White.—Dutch, White Transparent, Shilling's White.

GOOSEBERRIES.

White.—Whitesmith.

Yellow.—Early Sulphur.

Green.—Berry's Early Kent, Keepsake.

(The grower says "in 1886 though prices were low, I cleared £120 an acre from Berry's Kent alone.")

Red.—Crown Bob, Lancashire Lad, Whinham's Industry, Warrington.

RASPBERRIES.

Baumforth's Seedlings. Carter's Prolific, Filbasket, Norwich Wonder, Superlative, Hornet.

AUTUMN RASPBERRIES.

Yellow Four Seasons, Perpetual de Billiard.

(These should be cut down in February, and their summer growth thinned out.)

STRAWBERRIES.

La Grosse Sucre, Vicomtesse Hericaut de Thury, Noble, Royal Sovereign, Sir Joseph Paxton, Dr. Hogg, President, Waterloo, Latest of All.

CHAPTER XII.

LARGE FRUITS.

APPLES—*(Pyrus Malus)*.

The apple is essentially a fruit of the colder and more temperate regions of the globe, over which it is almost universally spread and cultivated. It is supposed by some to attain a great age. Haller mentions some trees in Hereford·shire that attained 1,000 years and were highly prolific ; but Knight considers 200 years as the ordinary duration of a healthy tree grafted on a crab stock and planted in a strong tenacious soil. The apple was probably introduced into Britain by the Romans, among whom it was a favourite fruit.

There are over 1,400 varieties in cultivation. Many of the better sorts of English apples were probably introduced at first from the continent.

The apple-tree thrives best in a rich deep loam, but it will thrive in any soil provided it is not too wet or too dry. It succeeds best in situations sheltered from the north and east, and which are neither high nor remarkably low. It is being extensively planted on the continent, and in Tasmania and Australia ; and it has been grown extensively for many years in North America, where they are still increasing the area of land devoted to its culture.

In order to keep possession of our markets, and to hold our own against the imported apples, it is necessary to increase the average quality of our apples put upon the market. This can only be done by limiting the number of varieties planted to a few of the best, and by planting a greater number of trees of each variety selected; by "grading" the fruit and sending only the "best" and "seconds" to market. Also by manuring more liberally the trees in bearing as they increase in age.

The habit of raising apple-trees from pips, or seed, must be abandoned so far as the generality of small gardens are concerned; that is one great source of the many comparatively worthless varieties of apples now in cultivation.

It is much better to buy young trees from nurserymen of repute, because such trees are best in every sense; healthy stocks only will have been used, scion and stock will be chosen on account of their adaptability to each other, their union will be most perfect because of having been grafted by the most experienced and practiced hands. As the trees are intended and expected to be fruitful for several generations, this is a more important matter than it appears at first sight. A tree grafted by our own hands is naturally very interesting, but it is not likely to be so satisfactory to our descendants; and there is great probability that the amateur grafter is responsible for many of the wretched and decrepit fruit trees in our gardens and orchards.

Stocks vary very much and greatly influence the growth, character, and fruitfulness of the trees established upon them. The Dwarf French Paradise induces an early and prolific fruitfulness, but it is not conducive to longevity. The broad-leaved Paradise is more robust and generally less precocious than the former, and is suitable for bushes and dwarf standards. The Nonsuch is suited for dwarf trees; it is robust, emits roots from buds on the stem below the soil and so is a surface-rooter, and is not prone to send out tap-roots. The Crab is most suitable for orchard standards.

The soil should be, as far as possible, a deep loam containing some lime, potash, and phosphoric acid; nitrogen may be added as opportunity permits, Soil that will grow good crops of wheat and roots will usually grow good crops of apples.

The ground ought to be drained if it is wet or near the water-level; and it should be broken up or trenched to a good depth some considerable time before planting. If it is inconvenient to trench the soil entirely, large holes should be excavated for each tree, considerably larger than the roots require when spread out. The holes should be eighteen inches to two feet deep. Let some of the top good soil be returned into these, and filled to such height (when pressed down) as will leave the trees about the same depth in the soil when planted as they were before, which depth will be indicated by an earth-mark around the stem of each plant or tree.

In planting, let the roots be carefully spread upon the soil regularly and nearly horizontally all round. Be sure to have the tree in the centre of each hole. Place some fine soil among the roots carefully, then some over the roots, and press the soil with the feet. Keep adding more soil and pressing it firmly until

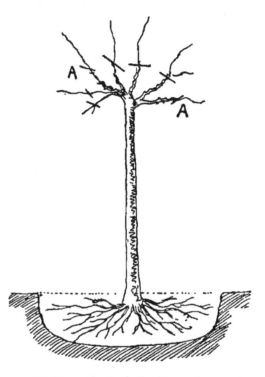

Right method of planting a tree and of shortening its branches.

the hole is filled. Finish off by forming a shallow saucer-like depression from the circumference of the new soil to the centre, for the purpose of retaining water when necessary to apply it. This is most requisite in the case of all trees if they are large, but not necessary for small trees.

If the soil is dry at the time of planting, as it sometimes is in autumn, a good watering may be given and a mulching of manure spread over the surface as far as the roots extend.

Each tree ought to be supported in some way against the loosening influence of the wind, because trees that are loose in the soil cannot obtain a firm grip with their roots, and do not root freely.   The best plan is to drive a strong and durable stake (stout bamboos are the best) firmly into each hole or position before the tree is planted.   By doing this there is no danger of injuring the top or stem of the tree with the mallet or hammer, or of driving the stake through any of the principal roots.   The stake should be an inch or two from the centre of the hole in order that the stem of the tree itself may be in the exact centre.

Strong and tarred twine or string forms the most satisfactory tying material, and a band or collar of some kind should be first placed round the stem of the tree; then the tar twine ought to be passed twice round the collar, then twisted twice or three times between the stem of the tree and the stake, and finally made secure round the stake.

Before each tree is planted, all the roots ought to be examined and any bruised or broken ones smoothed off with a sharp knife, each cut to have a sharp slope upwards and outwards, the wounds will then heal more quickly and be less liable to decay, and the new roots which are formed will have a start in the right direction.

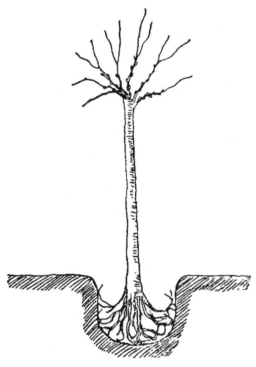

Wrong method of planting a tree.

Most trees are better for having their branches shortened more or less after being transplanted, but the amount of pruning to be done will be governed by circumstances.   Some good practitioners think that all stone fruits, especially plums, should be left unpruned, but I think a careful and even balancing of active roots and branches is the wisest policy.

Many trees have been killed through over-pruning, and some have been ruined because they were not pruned at all. Generally it is quite safe to prune to plump and living buds shortly after transplanting a tree, and the number of buds to be left, and subsequent leaves and shoots to be nourished, will depend upon the number and vitality of the roots belonging to the tree to be operated on.

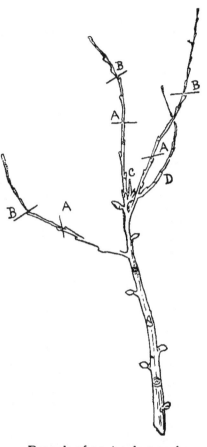

Branch pruning is one of the most misunderstood of all gardening operations. Many persons suppose that the mere act of pruning will make a tree fruitful. Pruning, rightly performed, can only be an aid to fruitfulness, and cannot, of itself, make a tree bear fruit.

There are three chief reasons for pruning :—first, to give a tree a particular form or shape ; second, to limit it in size ; third, to prevent over-crowding of leaves and branches ; the latter is the method that is the chief cause of fruit production. A fourth reason for pruning exists, viz :—to encourage the production of branches.

Branch of an Apple-tree bearing flower-buds. A A A show pruning too severely and the encouragement of more shoots. B B B shows more judicious pruning and the encouragement of more flower-buds.

In gardens, the system of pruning carried out is too frequently of the latter kind, quite unintentionally.

If a tree is in vigorous health it is imprudent to attempt to prevent that tree from extending itself in the natural way ; to do so will be productive of evil—more and inferior wood—and not of good—abundance of fruit.

The more we prune a healthy tree the more it will grow, until it becomes a mass of barren spurs or of worthless branches.

The way to obtain fruit in abundance and of fine quality, is to keep the trees healthy and well nourished; allow them as much extension of branch as is convenient, and keep each branch and shoot and spur so far from its neighbour that each leaf upon the tree will obtain a full share of sunshine and fresh air during its period of existence.

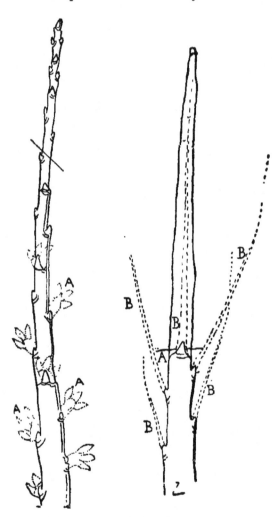

A   Pruning for fruit.

B   Pruning for wood.

To this end then, the science of pruning must be exercised. Keep the branches of a standard or orchard tree so wide apart that a man can easily move among the branches; of a dwarf or bush tree that he can get his head and shoulders between the branches; and the branches of an espalier or wall tree so far apart that the leaves upon one branch or spur do not shade the leaves upon its neighbour; which means that the branches should be from a foot to eighteen inches apart — according to circumstances, and the spurs on each branch from five to nine inches apart.

It is clear that one of the most important processes of pruning is the proper thinning out of the branches, and this is best done when the leaves are on ; we can then see better the amount of thinning required, the wounds heal more quickly, and the sap is diverted into other channels where it will be more beneficial. It is nonsense to suppose that the trees will bleed, as many unthinking and unobservant persons state.

Apples thinned ; fine fruit.   Apples not thinned ·
                                        small fruit.

If the trees are looked over at the beginning of July, and again at the end of August or early in September, and all superfluous shoots removed, the side shoots shortened to five or six leaves, any old snags removed, and a branch here and there where necessary, there will be little pruning required in winter.

The winter pruning will consist of shortening the leading shoots a little, cutting the side shoots to a bud or two below or nearer the branch than where they were cut at the first summer pruning, and removing any dead or over-crowding branch or spur.

Old and worn-out trees may be much improved in vigour and fruitfulness by annually removing any dead wood, encouraging the production of young wood thinly and evenly distributed over the trees, and by applying mulchings of manure and doses of liquid manure in summer or winter.

APRICOT.—*(Prunus Armeniaca)*.

The apricot is a fruit of the plum tribe, and was intro-duced into England in 1548. Some consider the apricot the most delicate of all our hardy fruits. It is used for tarts, both green and ripe; it is also preserved with sugar in both these states, and is sometimes dried as a sweetmeat. The apricot is an important article of food in the North-West Himalayas; and oil for lamps and cooking purposes is expressed from the kernels.

The tree in this country requires to be grown against a warm wall in a favourable and sunny district. It does not bear well the extremes of heat and cold, wet and drought, to which it is sometimes subject with us; hence the frequency of the loss of branches and of unhealthy trees.

If it is protected with a glass coping, or grown in an un-heated greenhouse, the tree is usually happy and prosperous, probably on account of the shelter it receives and the better maturity of the wood.

In Worcestershire, the apricot is commonly grown against cottages, where it is nearly annually laden with its golden and delicious fruit, and paying. in scores of instances, the rent of the cottage for the year. The climate is genial, the soil warm, and not too wet and cold, as in many districts.

The apricot fruits chiefly upon spurs and upon thoroughly ripened wood of moderate strength of the previous year.

The main branches should be widely distributed over the wall, and the side branches laid in between at wide intervals. Upon these latter fruit-spurs will form, and these should be prevented from being too close together by timely disbudding in the spring, when the bursting wood-buds on the shoots—the front part—immediately facing the operator ought to be removed with finger and thumb, and a few of the other buds on the upper and lower sides of the shoots, leaving the young growths about four inches apart alternately above and below. All buds between the shoots and the wall should be entirely removed Disbudding is a most valuable operation, and is the first and most important in the work of managing the growth of fruit trees. When this is properly carried out there is little necessity for the use of the knife, beyond the removal in autumn of exhausted fruit-bearing wood; these remarks apply especially to peach trees. But disbudding is equally important for vines, plums, pears and trained apples; and an acquaintance with, and mastery of, this work is one of the most important rungs in the ladder that reaches to success in fruit culture.

CHERRY.—*(Prunus Cerasus)*.

Besides being prized for its fruit the cherry is also a very ornamental tree, and is much cultivated for this object in gardens.

It is a native of most temperate countries of the northern hemisphere. It is generally said that the first of the present cultivated sorts was introduced about the time of Henry VIII., and was originally planted at Sittingbourne, in Kent. Pliny says that the cherry was introduced into Britain about A.D. 46, and at some of the ruined abbeys and baronial castles there are found cherry trees, chiefly black ones, which have attained the height of 60 or 80 feet, and produce great quantities of fruit.

The cherry is said to have been sent to Rome from Armenia by Lucullus, when engaged in the war against Mithridates (B.C. 74); and the word cherry is believed to be a corruption of Cerasus, the name of an ancient town on the Euxine or Black Sea. The gum that exudes from the bark is in many respects equal to gum-arabic, and is considered very nutritive. Hasselquist informs us that during a siege more than 100 men were kept alive for nearly two months without any other sustenance than a little of this gum, which they occasionally took into their mouths and suffered gradually to dissolve.

The bird-cherry (*prunus padus*) is a very ornamental tree in shrubberries, and its fruit is greedily eaten by birds.

The culture of cherries is not a profitable undertaking, unless they are grown so extensively as to be worth while protecting them from the birds, or to such an extent as to not miss those that are destroyed by them. Where only a few are required for home consumption, it will be best to plant one or two trees against a wall, where they can easily be protected by nets. Isolated standard trees are sometimes protected with netting if the trees are not large, but the protection is rather imperfect.

In the summer of 1890, I saw a cherry tree in a garden at Cawston, in Norfolk, apparently perfectly protected by a framework covered with close netting ; but, alas ! a blackbird had found his way in to the fruit and was having a delicious feast.   I do not know the fate of that blackbird but I can imagine the feelings of the owner of the cherries.

The management of cherries upon walls is similar to that advised for apricots—disbudding in spring, pinching to five or six leaves in summer, and judicious thinning out where required, and cutting the spurs closer back in winter.

Morello cherries are not so liable to the depredations of birds, and may be grown, with a view to profit, both as dwarf bushes in the open and on walls that are unsuitable for plums, apricots, pears, &c.

PEACH.—*(Prunus Persica)*.

Perhaps the peach cannot properly be considered a hardy fruit, and therefore not exactly in place in this book ; but as doubtless some readers may have one or more peach trees in their gardens, or are very desirous of growing peaches on the open walls they possess, a few hints about the management of peach trees may be acceptable.

The culture of the peach out-of-doors is not successful in many districts north of the Trent, but south of that river there are few places where good crops cannot be obtained, under careful management, from trees grown on walls.

The best aspects for peach trees are south, south-east, or south-west.   The roots ought not to be allowed to go more than two feet deep.   A firm border of loamy soil, with a good admixture of old mortar, will suit the peach tree admirably. Shoots varying in strength from the thickness of a quill to that of an ordinary cedar wood pencil are the kind to aim at obtaining ; they will be well nourished, well ripened, and fruitful.

Disbud in spring with a bold hand ; few amateurs do enough in this way ; many are afraid and do not do any. About five out of six of the young shoots want removing with finger and thumb as soon as they appear upon their parent shoot.   Leave just sufficient to furnish the fruit-bearing wood for the coming year, and a few pinched back to four or five leaves near the fruit and beyond it in order to draw the sap to the fruit.

As the shoots that are left to grow, for extending the tree where requisite and for producing fruit next year, increase in length, they ought to be neatly fastened near the wall and at about six inches apart from shoot to shoot. I know that few people will leave them at this distance apart, but I hope they will keep as near to this distance as they can ; then those shoots will not be overcrowded, the leaves will have plenty of air and light, and the wood will be of the best quality under the circumstances and most capable of passing through the winter uninjured and of producing fruit the following year.

As soon as the fruit is ripe and cleared from the tree, all the old wood that has borne the fruit should be cut out, and more space left for the young shoots that are to produce fruit the following year. Give the trees heavy syringings with water to clear the foliage of dirt and insect pests, and thus enable them to go on manufacturing embryo flowers and fruit for development the next year into the large, juicy, and luscious fruit that only a *good* peach can be.

PEAR.—*(Pyrus communis)*.

The cultivation of choice dessert pears in this country is essentially one of some uncertainty ; because the pear requires a warm season in which to attain its greatest excellence with us. Only our very best samples will compare favourably with those now imported from California, the Channel Islands, and France.

A judicious selection of varieties and careful choice of sites and aspects—in conjunction with skilful culture—will do much towards the production of good crops of fine fruit ; whereas carelessness and indifference is sure to promote comparative failure.

Mr. John Wright, in his excellent essay on profitable fruit-growing, says :—" Pears are more of a luxury than a necessity, but a most refreshing and wholesome luxury in large demand by a great and important section of the community." I think few persons will deny that proposition. From Midsummer to Christmas there is always a large demand .for good pears, and, too frequently, the prices are quite prohibitive.

The quince is a good stock upon which to graft most varieties of pears for ordinary garden culture ; but for large standards in orchards that have to withstand gales it is usually better to use the " free " or pear stock.

The procedure in respect to planting and pruning is precisely similar to that given for apples. When grown as pyramids, dwarf bushes, espaliers, cordons, and against walls, a little protection from frost can easily be applied to pears when in flower. A few small boughs of yew, box, laurel, spruce, or silver fir can easily be fixed among the pear branches, and the little protection thus given for a week or two often makes all the difference between having a good crop of fruit and no fruit.

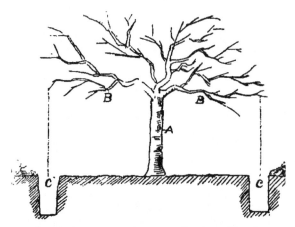

Manner of opening a trench around a tree for the purposes of root-pruning, root-lifting, and transplanting.

Similar protecting branches of evergreens may be used to pears against walls, and also to peaches, apricots and plums when in flower, if there is no better means of protection at hand.

Good varieties for growing as cordons are Beurré Superfine, Doyenne du Comice, Glou Morceau, Josephéne de Malines, Louise Bonne de Jersey, Chaumontel. Marie Louise, Passe Colmar, Princess, and Winter Nelis.

Suitable pears for walls with south aspect are :— Thompson's, Winter Nelis, Louise Bonne de Jersey, Beurré Rance, Beurré Bosc, Pitmaston Duchesse, Glou Morceau,

Marie Louise, Easter Beurré, Beurré d'Amanlis, Knight's Monarch, Gansel's Bergamot, Bergamot d'Esperen, Brown Beurré, and Beurré Perran.

For a wall facing west :—Williams' Bon Chretien, Doyenne du Comice, Beurré Diel, Marechal de la Cour, Louise Bonne de Jersey, Beurré Clairgeau, Beurré Giffard, Beurré d'Amanlis, and Josephìne de Malines, are good varieties. I have not mentioned Jargonelle because it is so well known, and succeeds so well in almost any position.

Many pears are spoiled through being improperly gathered ; they are pulled from the tree either too soon or are allowed to remain on too long. If plucked too soon the fruit shrivels before it ripens ; if left too long on the tree some varieties become utterly worthless ; Jargonelle and Williams' Bon Chretien are familiar examples of the latter case, Williams' being dry and juiceless and the Jargonelles decayed in the centre.

The gathering of pears at the proper time requires close personal attention, and no general rule in regard to date of gathering can be fixed upon. There is one fairly safe test to indicate when the fruit may be properly gathered, viz. :—by raising, with the hand, each fruit from the perpendicular

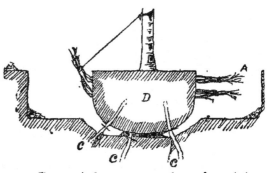

Roots tied up to save them from injury whilst workmen get under the ball of the tree to sever the tap-roots C.C.C.

(or natural) position to the horizontal ; and if the fruit is quite fit to gather it will part easily from the tree at the junction between the stalk and branch. If the fruit does not then part freely from the tree it is much better to wait a few days.

In order to prolong the season of pears, it is recommended to make two or three gatherings from each tree, which proves a great advantage ; removing each fruit as it arrives at the stage of ripeness as advised above.

A few words here upon root-pruning or root-lifting will not be out of place, because pear trees usually require the operation as much and as often as other fruit trees. The advantages of careful root-pruning are five-fold : it induces fruitfulness ; improves the flavour of the fruit ; is preventive of canker and gumming to a great extent; prevents the formation of gross and worthless shoots ; and reduces the labour of branch-pruning.

In commencing to lift or prune the roots of a fruit tree we must proceed in every way as though we were about to transplant it to another position, taking the same care of all the roots as we would in actually transplanting it. Proceed by digging a trench about two feet deep and nearly as far from

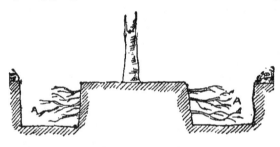

Roots exposed.

the stem as will be equal to the radius or length of the branches. Let the trench be eighteen to twenty-four inches wide. It must be clearly understood that the larger the tree is, the greater is the necessity for opening a larger trench at a proportionately greater distance from the stem ; this is for the convenience of having room to move about when the operator has to descend into the trench for the purpose of working more carefully among the roots, and to get at any tap-roots or anchor-roots that descend nearly perpendicularly from below the ball of soil and near the stem of the tree.

Gradually remove, with a fork, the soil from among the roots all round the tree, and keep carefully working towards the stem until nearly all the roots have been found. In some cases further digging and forking is unnecessary, but frequently it is advisable to tie the roots carefully into small bundles as the work proceeds, and occasionally to tie them upwards to the stem or branches, in order that they may be more out of harm's way and leave more freedom for working.

Having found the tap-roots let them be severed with a sharp knife, saw, or long-handled chisel and mallet. The lower part of the root should be got out if possible ; but if this cannot be done, then as much of it as possible should be cut away, and a tile or slate should be placed under the root

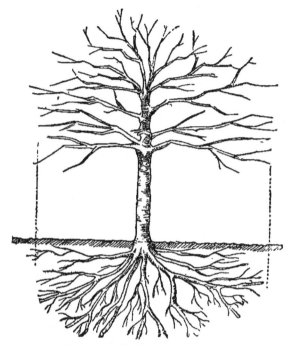

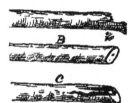

A. Root chopped through with spade.

B. Root with end properly trimmed.

C. Root with end wrongly trimmed.

Right method of root-pruning, and preservation of fibrous roots.

already cut, to induce new roots to assume a horizontal position. We must next proceed to examine the ordinary roots, and cut smoothly with a sharp knife the ends of all the roots that were injured, taking care that the cut be upwards and outwards.

The roots may now be re-planted in the usual way, placing each set of roots in their own layer of soil and not altogether at one level. Proceed as with re-planting a tree, and finish off in the manner recommended in planting fruit trees in the matter of mulching, &c.

October is the best month for root-pruning or root-lifting trees.

PLUM.—*(Prunus domestica).*

The plum does not take the same rank as the peach or pear as a dessert fruit, but there is a likelihood that, as the drying of plums becomes an industry of greater value, dessert plums will assume an importance far beyond the position they at present occupy.

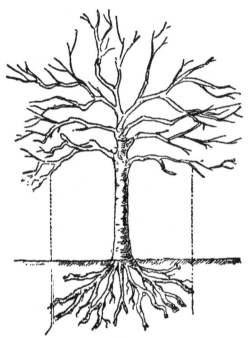

Wrong method of root-pruning and decay of main roots through commencing too near the tree.

Plums are a profitable crop in suitable positions and localities, and are often worth from £50 to £80 per acre. Pershore, Victoria, and Rivers' Early Prolific are reliable and heavy croppers, and are favourite market varieties. The Czar, the Mallard, Curlew, Mitchelson's, New Early Orleans, Prince Englebert, Belle de Septembre and Monarch are also free bearing varieties.

They succeed well as dwarf standards on grass, or on cultivated land and in gardens, and also on walls of all aspects except due north. Good varieties for growing on walls are Transparent Gage, Oulin's Golden Gage, Purple Gage, Jefferson, Coe's Golden Drop, Belle de Septembre, Victoria, Pond's Seedling, Reine Claude de Bavay, and Magnum Bonum (white and yellow).

In the districts of Evesham and Pershore several thousands of acres are planted with plums, mainly Victoria, Early Prolific, and Pershore ; and hundreds of tons of plums are daily despatched from those stations, and others in the district, from the middle of August to the middle of September.

Plum trees, grown as dwarf standards, require very little pruning after their heads are well furnished with branches, and only require to be examined occasionally and any branches that cross each other, or are crowding, to be removed. The centre of each tree should be kept open to admit light and air freely.

Trees grown upon walls must be managed and pruned as advised for apricots, always remembering that timely disbudding in spring wins more than half the battle in regard to their successful management, and should be followed in summer with nailing in the leading shoots and judicious shortening of the side shoots.

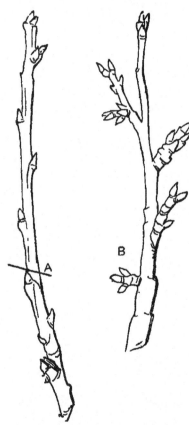

When trees are bearing heavy crops of fruit they ought to be well supplied with food, and this is best given as surface dressings or mulchings, and by means of liquid manure.

Deep digging about fruit trees should be avoided, and crops that are exhausting in their nature ought not to be planted near fruit-trees.

If the soil is naturally deficient in lime a liberal supply must be given to all kinds of stone-fruits and apple-trees; and very often lime must be afforded even when the soil may naturally contain a large percentage of it, for the reason that the lime may be unavailable, or out of the reach of the roots of the trees, the trees thus languishing and the crops failing for want of that which is

A   Method of pruning side-shoot of Plum.

B   Natural fruit-spurs of Plum.

present in abundance, but which they cannot avail themselves of.

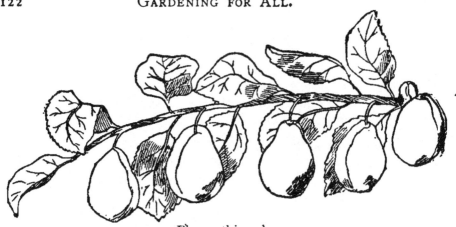

Plums, thinned.

The cultural details and other information which I have attempted to clearly impart, and which I trust may be of service to many readers, are based upon over thirty years daily practical experience and observation, and of notes and memoranda collected in various parts of England from the successful practice of others as well as of my own practice; and I heartily endorse the sentiments recently expressed by Mr. Gladstone, who ~~recently~~ said, " There is an immense deal to be done in this country by drawing forth the bounty of old mother earth. Undoubtedly, the advances of machinery had been astonishing, but, as regards garden cultivation and small cultivation, there is more room than ever for both adding to the store of the beautiful products of nature and consolidating the advantages of rural life."

Plums, not thinned.

SELECTIONS OF VARIETIES FOR QUALITY AND
PRODUCTIVENESS.

Apples (Dessert).—Irish Peach, Cox's Orange Pippin, Claygate Pearmain, Worcester Pearmain, King of the Pippins, Scarlet Nonpareil, Brownlee's Russet, Court Pendû Plat. *Cooking or Dessert.*—Duchess of Oldenburg, Blenheim Orange, Cox's Pomona, Herefordshire Pearmain. *Culinary.*—Keswick Codlin, Lord Grosvenor, Stirling Castle, Ecklinville Seedling, Warner's King, Lord Derby, Small's Admirable, Lane's Prince Albert, Bramley's Seedling, Dumelow's Seedling, and Early White Transparent.

Apricots.—Blenheim (Shipley), Early Moor Park, Moor Park, Royal, Peach, Hemskirk.

Peaches —Early Beatrice, Royal George, Mignon Grosse, Noblesse, Hale's Early, Walburton Admirable, Pitmaston Orange (Nectarine), Victoria (Nectarine).

Cherries.—Early Rivers, Black Tartarian, Governor Wood, Elton, May Duke, Kentish Bigarreau.

Pears.—Citron des Carmes, Jargonelle, Beurre Giffard Clapp's Favourite, Williams' Bon Chretien, Beurre d'Amanlis, Beurre Superfin, Louise Bonne de Jersey, Beurré Hardy, Marie Louise, Marechal de la Cour, Beurre Bosc, Doyenne du Comice, Pitmaston Duchesse, Marie Louise d'Uccle, Beurre Diel, Winter Nelis, Josephine de Malines. *Pears for Stewing.*—Catillac, Vicar of Winkfield, Gilogil, Uvedale's St. Germain.

Plums (Dessert).—Belgian Purple, Oulin's Golden Gage, Reine Claude Gage, Jefferson, Coe's Golden Drop, Angelina Burdett, Denniston's Superb Gage, Reine Claude de Bavay, Early Transparent Gage. *Culinary.*—Rivers' Early Prolific, Stint, The Mallard, The Czar, Victoria, Pershore, Prince Engelbert, Belle de Septembre, Pond's Seedling, Grand Duke, Diamond, Monarch.

CHAPTER XIII.

INSECT PESTS:—Their prevention and destruction.

GREEN FLY OR ROSE APHIS.—*(Siphonophora rosa)*.

Most of the female aphis bring forth their young alive, two young having been produced in half-an-hour. Some broods of female aphis always produce their young alive, others always lay eggs. The young which are born alive begin to produce young in four to eight days.

One female being once impregnated, her progeny bring forth young without further impregnation for many generations, and the progeny of one aphis after the end of one hundred days is said to possibly amount to 3,200,000 !

About the middle of September the last generation are produced, male and female; they pair and eggs are deposited in due course. These eggs hatch in spring, when all that are hatched are wingless females, which produce their young alive in a few days. After several changes of skin they become perfect insects either with or without wings; winged ones fly to fresh plants and found new colonies. Some females **hybernate** during the winter.

The species of aphis just mentioned attacks many kinds of plants, but there are other species which seem to be confined to special kinds of trees; for example :—Aphis cerasi exists mainly upon the young shoots of the cherry; aphis persicœ, upon the peach and nectarine; aphis pruni, upon the plum and damson.

Under glass all kinds of aphis may be kept in subjection by timely fumigation, but plants out of doors cannot conveniently be fumigated, and they must be kept clean by spraying and syringing.

A good solution consists of boiling a quarter of a pound of Quassia chips in one gallon of water for twenty minutes and adding two ounces of soft soap. For aphis upon the cherry, peach or plum, an extra ounce of soap may be requisite.

An emulsion of soft soap and petroleum is very efficacious against many insect pests, and, if properly made and applied, will not be injurious to the plants. This may easily be made by boiling together, and constantly stirring whilst boiling and cooling, one pound of soft soap, half-a-pint of petroleum, and one quart of water; this will be sufficient to make sixteen gallons of insecticide for green aphis, or eight gallons for plum and cherry aphis.

Spraying with Paris green at the rate of one ounce to sixteen gallons of water has also been found very efficacious. Paris green, when properly applied, is a great boon to the fruit grower.

RED SPIDER.—*(Tetranychus telarius).*

This is a minute insect very troublesome to many kinds of plants, especially in hot and dry weather. Although called a " spider " it is in reality a mite, and they differ in size and colour according to variety. Heat and drought are favourable to their propagation and general well-being ; cold and wet are unfavourable.

Applications of clear water will usually keep them in subjection, but where they have obtained a foothold stronger measures must be applied for their complete dislodgment.

Spraying with Paris green, at the rate of one ounce to sixteen gallons of water, has been quite efficacious upon many out-door trees and crops, particularly gooseberries, currants, plums and apples. For delicate plants in greenhouses a safe mixture to use is sulphide of potassium, at the rate of half-an-ounce to one gallon of water.

Another and more homely mixture is two ounces of soft soap to one gallon of water.

The solution of sulphide of potassium is also efficacious against mildew, and tomato disease upon tomato leaves if properly applied.

THRIPS

are very partial to the foliage of azaleas, vines, orchids, &c., and should not receive any quarter. Frequent and timely fumigations are very beneficial, and the washes advised for aphis will suffice to destroy thrips.

BLACK CURRANT MITE.—*(Phytoptis).*

This mite infests and destroys the buds of black currants; and, although the insect is scarcely visible to the naked eye, its presence is easily detected during the winter months by the abnormally large appearance of the buds upon the shoots. These buds are large and round, and to the uninitiated, appear as though they were about to yield an extra large crop of fruit ; but, as a matter of fact, little or no growth comes from these buds, for the simple reason that the mites have been feeding upon the embryo leaves and flowers.

Where bushes are only slightly affected the mite may be eradicated by carefully picking off and burning all affected buds. Spraying during the spring months with the emulsion of soft soap and petroleum will destroy many mites as they descend to the ground. The same should be done in autumn after the fruit is gathered and about the fall of the leaf, when they are ascending the trees. In cases where the plantations are large and the attack very bad, time and money will be saved by destroying and burning the plantation and cropping the ground with something else for a few years.

THE GOOSEBERRY AND CURRANT SAWFLY.

This sawfly emerges from the chrysalis state about the end of March or beginning of April. Eggs are laid, which hatch in a week or ten days, and the young caterpillars commence feeding upon the tender leaves where they were hatched, and feed until full grown. They then descend to the soil, change into a chrysalis, and emerge again the perfect fly during the summer ; our trees are thus liable to two attacks during the season.

Spraying with Paris green at the rate of one ounce to twelve gallons of water has been found to rid the trees entirely of them. Spraying with Hellebone powder has also been found effective, but more expensive. A deadly mixture may also

be composed of one pound of Quassia chips boiled in one
gallon of water, twelve ounces of Carbolic soap, and half-an-
ounce of Paris green to ten gallons of water ; this may be
applied by means of a sprayer or fine syringe.

Some dust their bushes over with fine lime, which is
sometimes an effective agent.

The mixture of Paris green and soap is apt to make
spraying or syringing difficult, by stopping up the orifice in
the nozzle ; therefore sometimes it becomes necessary to use
the Paris green alone with water in the proportions of one
ounce to sixteen gallons of water.

THE MAGPIE MOTH.—*(Abraxas grossulariata).*

The caterpillars of this moth are very destructive to the
foliage of gooseberries. They are usually hatched about
August, " feed for a while, and then spin together the edges
of a gooseberry leaf, having first taken the precaution of
making the leaf fast to its twig by numerous silken cables,
which prevents the possibility of its falling when dehiscence
(separation of leaf from branch) takes place in the autumn.
In the little cradle thus woven the infant caterpillar sleeps as
securely as the sailor in his hammock. Snow storms and
wintry winds are matters of indifference to him, but no sooner
have the gooseberry bushes begun to assume their livery of
green in the spring, than instinct informs him that food is
preparing to satisfy his appetite, so he cuts an opening in his
hanging cradle, emerges, and begins to eat." Many descend
to the soil and take shelter beneath, to emerge in spring and
ascend the bushes.

The remedies advised for the previous insect will be
right for this ; to which may be added the removal and
charring of the soil under the affected bushes, and the
application of lime over the surface of the soil beneath the
trees.

SLUG-WORM.—*(Selandria cerasi).*

This pest is the larvæ of a saw-fly, and is found frequently
upon the leaves of pears and cherries. The best remedy is to
pick off the affected leaves and burn them, and to syringe
frequently with lime-water.

WINTER MOTH.—*(Cheimatobia brumata)*.

The caterpillar of the winter moth is very destructive to the leaves and flowers of apple and plum trees as well as to other kinds.

The female moths, being furnished with rudimentary wings only, cannot fly, and therefore have to creep up the stems of the trees in order to deposit their eggs near the buds upon the shoots. The period of egg laying may begin at the end of September and proceed to the end of December.

The eggs are hatched as the spring comes round, and the baby caterpillars at once commence to feed upon the young unfolding leaves. They go on feeding until full grown, when they descend to the ground and take refuge there under clods, stones, and among grass roots, or burrow into the soil and form earthen coccoons.

Each female lays 200 to 300 eggs, and the chief thing to do is to prevent those eggs being laid. This can be aecomplished by placing grease bands around the trees, employing, in all cases, something to prevent the grease coming in direct contact with the bark. Grease-proof paper is the material generally used. These bands are first fastened round each tree, then the grease is smeared nearly all over the paper. I have seen the bands quite covered with male and female moths; and later insects use the dead bodies of their comrades as bridges to carry them safely across the otherwise fatal ground.

Care must be taken that there are no crevices left between the greased paper and the tree; and when the greased paper is covered with moths, or the grease has become too hard to hold the moths, more fresh grease must be applied.

In addition to catching the moths in this way, means ought to be taken to destroy any caterpillars that may be hatched in the trees notwithstanding the grease-bands. For this purpose the trees ought to be syringed or sprayed, before the buds expand, with the extract of ten pounds of Quassia chips, to which may be added seven pounds of carbolic soap and five ounces of Paris green, the whole to be mixed with 100 gallons of water. Sprayings afterwards, at intervals of three weeks, with Paris green and water at the rate of one ounce to sixteen gallons, will usually keep the trees in a healthy condition. The latter is usually quite adequate.

The stems and branches of apple, plum, pear, and cherry trees ought always to be cleansed from moss and lichen. A piece of old hoop-iron is a handy implement for scraping the trees with ; this operation should be followed by a good brushing with a broom, and then the stems ought to be whitewashed. If the trees are regularly cared for in this way they will be clean and practically free from insect pests.

The foregoing measures also effectively deal with the caterpillars of the Figure of 8 Moth, the Gipsy Moth, Lackey Moth, Small Ermine Moth, &c.

APPLE BLOSSOM WEEVIL.—*(Anthonomus pomorum)*.

This weevil is a cause of great mischief to apple trees, itself feeding upon the leaves, and its larvæ destroying the reproductive organs of the blossoms. More failures of the apple crop are due to this pest than it gets credit for.

The female weevil proceeds from bud to bud, pierces a small hole in the side of the bud, and deposits one egg in each bud. The egg hatches in a few days, and the maggot feeds at once upon the pistil and stamens. The buds cease to develope, turn brown, and shelter the maggot.

The remedies advised for the winter moth are suitable for destroying this pest, and for preventing its ravages.

AMERICAN BLIGHT OR WOOLLY APHIS.—*(Schizoneura Lanigera)*.

American blight may spread from tree to tree either by migration of the winged females, or it may be spread by means of the wind ; the latter conveying the cotton or wool in which may be lodged eggs or young aphis.

Dress the trees repeatedly (the affected parts) with spirits of wine, if on a small scale ; or with the petroleum emulsion if on a large scale. One dressing of either will not be sufficient ; dress again in May without touching young shoots or leaves.

MUSSEL SCALE.—*(Mytilaspis pomorum)*.

Apple trees are most subject to the attack of mussel scale ; pear trees are occasionally infested with the white pear scale, and the brown scale attacks various kinds of plants.

Spirits of wine or the petroleum emulsion may be brushed over the affected parts, and train oil is a popular remedy; any of the three may be applied with a painter's sash-brush.

RASPBERRY MAGGOT.—*(Lampronia rubiella)*.

This bright red maggot is found in the centre of the young growths, whose presence is usually first indicated by the flagging or withering of said growth. The maggot should be diligently sought for and destroyed; do not allow one to escape.

The young growths of raspberries are sometimes destroyed by a weevil. A white cloth, or a board or tray covered with some sticky material, should be held under the affected plants after dusk and the canes shaken, when the weevils will fall upon the tray or cloth and may be destroyed.

LARGE WHITE BUTTERFLY.—*(Pieris brassicæ)*.

The larvæ of this insect is so destructive that those who have kitchen gardens, or are interested in agriculture, should ruthlessly kill every cabbage butterfly that comes across them.

The first eggs are hatched in May, and a second brood makes its appearance in August. The Rev. J. G. Wood says—" If its numbers were not kept down by the ichneumon flies we should scarcely have a cabbage in England."

After the eggs are deposited, little can be done to destroy the caterpillars beyond dusting the plants with fine lime, watering overhead with lime-water, and hand-picking.

CABBAGE MOTH.—*(Hadena brassicæ)*.

Mr. Wood, writing of this pest, says—" That this moth subserves some good purpose is evident from the fact of its existence, but what that purpose may be is not easy to discover. The caterpillar of this moth is one of the most voracious herb-feeders in this country. It can eat almost any herb, but prefers those which belong to the cabbage tribe. As for those which are cultivated with solid masses of vegetation, such as the summer cabbage and the broccoli (cauliflower?), this larvæ is terribly destructive, burrowing through and through the very heart of the vegetable." Adopt the same remedies as for the white butterfly caterpillar.

TURNIP MOTH.—*(Agrotis segetum)*.

The caterpillar of this moth attacks auriculas, dahlias, asters, balsams, cabbage, cauliflowers, turnips, lettuce, radishes, beetroot, spinach, mangolds, &c. When very young the caterpillar feeds upon the leaves of some of the plants mentioned, and in that stage may be removed by hand-picking; but, when it grows larger, it descends towards the earth, fixes upon the upper portion of the root, just where it joins the stem, and there gnaws a groove completely round the stem, the entire plant often dying from the injury.

Rooks and moles feed upon these caterpillars. Various remedies may be suggested for destroying them, but none are both thoroughly effective and safe. Suggested remedies are:—watering with salt and water at the rate of one ounce of salt to one gallon of water; or with one pound of carbolic soap to sixteen gallons of water; tobacco water; or mixtures of petroleum emulsion. Search for the caterpillars near the affected plants.

DADDY-LONG-LEGS.—*(Tipula longicornis)*.

The larvæ of daddy-long-legs, or crane fly, is very destructive to many plants. In Worcestershire the larvæ is known as the "leather-jacket." The crane flies should be destroyed and the larvæ diligently sought for. Starlings are great aids in their destruction.

ASPARAGUS BEETLE.—*(Crioceris Asparagi)*.

The beetle and larvæ are very injurious to asparagus after it has passed the "cutting" stage, consuming the young leaves and green colouring of the stalks and branches, and causing their death. The insect may usually be found upon the plant in three different stages at the same time: eggs, maggots, and perfect beetles.

Syringing with petroleum emulsion at the rate of half-a-pint to six gallons of water usually destroys the eggs and maggots. Spraying with Paris green at the rate of one ounce to ten gallons of water will poison the beetles; or they may be shaken on to white cloths, or paper and then destroyed, or on to boards or trays covered with some sticky material.

Small birds are useful allies in combating the pest.

PEA AND BEAN WEEVIL.—*(Bruchus)*.

Seed peas and beans frequently contain the perfect insect at the time of sowing. All doubtful seed should be steeped for half-an-hour before sowing in a preparation of the petroleum emulsion at the strength of half-a-pint to two quarts of water. Dusting the growing crops freely with soot or lime, or both combined, will check the depredations of the beetle and encourage the crop. Spraying with Paris green, one ounce to twelve gallons of water, is a preventive.

TURNIP FLEA.—*(Phyllotreta nemorum)*.

The turnip flea is very injurious to turnips, radishes, and brassica generally when in the seedling stage of existence. Its ravages may be checked by spraying with Paris green, or dusting with soot or lime, as recommended for the pea weevil. Watering with liquid manure is objectionable to the flea, and promotes the growth of the plants. Spraying with petroleum emulsion is also a preventive ; apply at the rate of half-a-pint to ten gallons of water.

TURNIP FLY or NIGGER.—*(Athalia spinarum)*.

These flies do not taste the turnips but only come to them on family business : they deposit their eggs on the under side of the leaf, glueing them on the cuticle. The eggs hatch in about nine days and the young maggots at once commence feeding in right earnest. In an incredibly short space of time the green of the leaf is gone, and nothing is visible but the naked skeletons of veins, which the niggers do not choose to consume. A whole field of swedes is completely destroyed by these little maggots in a few days.

Spraying with Paris green at the rate of one ounce to sixteen gallons of water will destroy the maggots and save the crop, if done in time. Ducks may be turned into the field to consume the maggots, but Paris green must not be used in that case or the ducks will be poisoned.

CELERY FLY.—*(Tephritis onopordinis)*.

Two or more broods of the celery fly are likely to work great havoc among celery from June to November. The first attack should be watched for and the affected part of the leaf removed and burnt ; if this is done at the commencement of the season, any further attack may be obviated.

Where an attack is apprehended, or the fly and its larvæ is already present, a free use should be made of soot, salt, and wood ashes; also lime may be used with care. The main point to observe is to destroy each maggot on its first appearance.

BEET FLY.

The same measures should be adopted for this as for the celery fly, with the addition that a dressing of artificial manure, or a good application of liquid manure, will enable the beet or mangolds to outgrow the attack.

CABBAGE FLY.—(*Anthomyia brassicæ*).

This fly deposits eggs in the stem of the young cabbage or cauliflower near the ground. The eggs are hatched in a few days, and the maggots eat their way into the centre of the young stem. Many of the plants die, some survive. Soot and lime in contact with the stem prevents the laying of the eggs. Earthing high up enables the plants to form fresh roots above the parts injured by the maggots (when the eggs have been deposited) if the injury is not soon fatal. When the presence of this fly is suspected (or known to actually exist) in the garden or neighbourhood, the plants ought to be often dusted with soot when they are in the seed-bed, as well as protected and helped in the way previously suggested when planted out.

TURNIP-GALL WEEVIL.—(*Ceutorrhynchus sulcicollis*).

The larvæ of this insect is a frequent cause of the wart-like excrescences found on the roots of turnips and cabbages. The female weevil pierces a hole in the root or stem of the turnip or cabbage, and deposits an egg in each hole. The eggs hatch in a few days, and the maggot feeds and lives in the root until fully grown, when they eat their way out, descend into the ground, and turn into chrysalids.

Adopt same remedies as for the cabbage fly, and dip the roots of cabbages, &c., into a thin paste formed of cow manure, soot, and lime.

ANBURY OR CLUBBING

is caused by a fungus, and is best prevented by a long course of rotation—cropping and by a judicious use of gas-lime or quick-lime.

WIREWORM.—*(Elater linearis)*.

There is no royal road to success in the destruction of this scourge to the gardener and farmer, and the pest is most difficult to extirpate.

It is the larvæ of a beetle, and remains as a wireworm four or five years, when it changes into the pupal state to ultimately come forth the perfect beetle.

Good cultivation of the soil—which includes the frequent stirring of the soil—does much to reduce their numbers, because their feathered enemies find them more readily. Moles, pheasants, and rooks are said to feed upon them ; also starlings, blackbirds, thrushes, and partridges. Rape cake and rape dust is one of the best of baits for them, and by this means many acres of hops are protected from them. Carrots, turnips, potatoes, and beet are also good baits. The bait should be frequently examined and the wireworms destroyed.

ONION FLY.—*(Anthomyia ceparum)*.

The onion maggot is the larvæ of a fly who deposits her eggs upon the onions principally during May. It is a simple matter to prevent the eggs being deposited, and so prevent the mischief. This may be done by frequent dressings with soot and lime, or soot alone. The soot should be applied evenly all over each plant in the bed by means of a dredger, or some dredging material such as coarse muslin or wasp netting. Take a piece of such material eighteen inches or two feet square, place in it a spadeful of soot, pick up the material by its four corners, and shake the soot through the meshes carefully all over the onions ; do not miss one. Repeat the operation at intervals of about a week, to the end of May or beginning of June.

According as these dressings are frequently and effec-tively given, so will be the immunity of the crop from the attack of the maggot if the onion fly is in the vicinity. To insure the most perfect success, the onions ought to be sown before the middle of March.

CARROT FLY.—*(Psila rosæ)*.

Carrots are injured by the larvæ of the carrot-fly, who deposits her eggs about the top of the root. The preventive measures recommended for the onion maggot ought to be applied to the carrots, and at the same time. Keep the crown of the carrots nicely covered with soil ; and, if any carrots or onions appear to be affected, let them be at once pulled up and burned. Carrots sown early in July are not so liable to attack as those sown in spring.

CHAPTER XIV.

DRYING FRUITS, VEGETABLES, AND HERBS.

In these times of extremely low prices for nearly all kinds of produce from the garden, orchard, and farm—as a result of competition and abundant crops—all efforts ought to be directed towards checking any waste of " the fruits of the earth ; " first, by prevention of early decay ; and second, by treating them by processes that will most ensure their keeping in the greatest perfection for the longest period, and with the least possible loss of food constituents.

Probably the highest preservative qualities are attained by the process of evaporation, whereby the water is dispelled and the article undergoes certain important chemical changes which prevents fermentation and decay without reducing its food value.

In years like 1895, when there is great abundance of fruit of all kinds except pears, there has always been great waste, because the average prices did not pay for the cost of gathering and sending the fruit to market ; consequently some growers do not obtain much benefit as a result of seasons of abundance, the fruit being left to rot upon the trees and upon the ground, not even being ground up for cider !

Considering that many thousands of pounds sterling are annually paid in this country for imported dried and tinned fruits, it must be patent to the most superficial observer that there is something wrong somewhere, and that some portion of the wrong is here among ourselves and clearly traceable to our own neglect in allowing our superabundant fruit to be wasted, instead of drying and preserving it for future use.

All who *grow* fruit may *dry* fruit also if they choose. Evaporating machines may be obtained at prices varying from £6 10s. 0d. to £150, with a proportionate number of drying trays of from eight to two hundred and thirty-eight ; the latter with a drying capacity of 3,000lbs. (or about forty-five pots) of fresh apples in twenty-four hours.

Some attention has been given in this country to the subject of drying fruit and vegetables for several years, but much more remains to be done.   It is a subject which must, sooner or later, receive a large share of attention—especially of market gardeners and farmers, also some attention from gentlemen's gardeners, and caterers for large establishments such as hotels, boarding houses, public schools, hospitals, asylums, &c.   The apparatus is most simple in construction and easy to manage, and the whole process of successful drying of fruit and vegetables, by means of the " American " evaporator, may be carried out by any man or woman of ordinary intelligence.

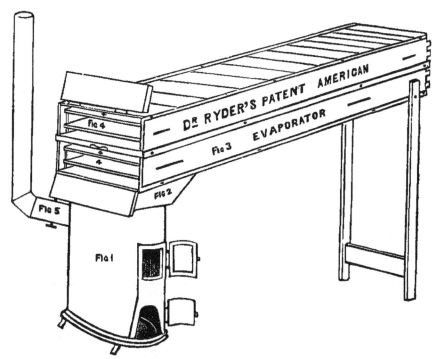

American Evaporator, No. 2

One of the pioneers and most successful of fruit dryers in this country is Mr. Trotter, head gardener to Mr. F. Ricardo, Bromesberrow Place, Ledbury. The greater part of Bromesberrow Place is in Worcestershire, the boundary line separating Worcestershire and Gloucestershire passing through a portion of the mansion itself; therefore, to Worcestershire belongs the honour of leading the van in this new and important branch of the industry of the production and preservation of fruits and vegetables.

Mr. Trotter has exhibited examples of dried apples, plums, damsons, cherries, pears, currants, apricots, figs, asparagus, tomatoes, French beans, peas, thyme, parsley, sage, mint, pennyroyal, &c., in various parts of the country, and has been awarded twenty-two first prizes, including six silver and two gold medals.

The machine in use at Bromesberrow Place is the "American" Evaporator, No. 2, and cost about £19. It occupies a space about twelve feet long, four feet broad, and eight feet high in a commodious and light shed where all the processes of peeling, coring, slicing, crystallising, drying and packing can easily and conveniently be carried on at the same time. The garden labourers do much of the work on days when the weather prevents them following their usual vocation, and such work is at once comfortable, pleasant, and profitable.

The clever invention for at once peeling, slicing, and coring apples is worked as simply as a hand sewing machine. The apple is placed upon the triple spindle, the knives brought into working contact with the screw shaft, six or seven turns of the handle, and the apple is peeled, cored, and sliced. Price, 18s.

All apples and tomatoes must be peeled before being placed into the evaporator, otherwise they will come out as *roasted* apples and tomatoes instead of the dried article. Mr. Trotter admits failure at first in that respect. He also says that other fruits and vegetables must be submitted to a lower temperature at first until the skin has begun to shrink.

The ripest fruit dries most quickly; fruit less ripe requires a longer period of time; this applies especially to apples and also to their respective varieties. Further, some varieties of apples give a larger per centage of weight after drying than other varieties.

The approximate drying temperatures, and length of time required, for the various fruits and vegetables are as follow :—

Whole Apples,	175 to 240	degrees F. ; 8 to 10 hours.					
Pears	212 „ 240	„	„		„	—	„
.. Plums	240 „ 300	„	„	6	„	10	„
Peaches	200 „ 212	„	„	2	„	3	„
„ Apricots	240 „ 250	„	„	2	„		„
„ Cherries	212 „ 220	„	„	4	„		„
Figs ..	200 „ 212			2	„	3	
Currants (Black)	180 „ 200	„	„	2	„	—	„
„ (Red)	180 „ 200	„	„	2	„	—	
Asparagus	150 „ 160	„	„	1	„	1½	„
French Beans	150 „ 160		„	¾	„	1	„
Tomatoes	200 „ 212		„	2	„	3	„
Peas	212 „ 220	„		1	„	1½	„
Thyme	150 „ 200	„	„	10	„	15 minutes.	
Parsley	150 „ 200	„	„	5	„	—	„
Sage	200 „ 220	„	„	10	„	15	„
Mint, same as for Parsley.							
Pennyroyal,	„						

Apple rings and " cored " apples require much less time than whole apples.

Mr. Trotter calculates that their evaporator consumes seventy-five pounds of coal in twenty-four hours, during which period about 400lbs. of " green " apples would have been dried, and he puts the total cost of drying at about sixpence per bushel. They dispose of their apple rings at fivepence and sixpence per pound, whole apples at eightpence and ninepence, and " cored " apples at tenpence per pound.

Small apples are necessarily more costly to " dry " than are larger and finer fruit. Fifty-six pounds of average sized apples yield about ten pounds of dried apple " rings," and these at fourpence per pound would be worth three shillings and fourpence, or six shillings and eightpence per hundredweight ; if we deduct one shilling for cost of drying it leaves five shillings and eightpence per hundredweight for the apples. Jelly is made from the parings and corings, which would add a little to the total value per hundredweight of the fruit.

Perhaps the whole *modus operandi* of fruit drying may best be given in Mr. Trotter's own words, and this is what he says :—

" In the following remarks I shall endeavour to give a clear description of an evaporating machine and the method of working the same successfully in this country. These statements are based upon practical experience, the writer having used The American Evaporator (Dr. Ryde's Patent) No. 2 during the past four years, and been awarded twenty-two prizes, including seven gold and silver medals, which fact will speak for itself respecting the excellence of the articles produced under the method hereafter described.

" Fruit drying, or, more properly, fruit evaporation, as a means of utilising surplus fruit in a plentiful year is an industry of great importance. American fruit-growers, like ourselves, have suffered from the evil of glutted markets, and have, with characteristic energy, applied themselves to solve the difficulty of utilising their surplus fruit in such a way as to turn every pound of it to profitable use and of monetary value, with the result that fruit drying has been an industry in that country for more than twenty years. It is a method whereby fruit, &c., can be cheaply preserved in a good and saleable condition for several years, thus making the producer independent (to a certain extent) of the circumstances of time and place, and enabling him to place his fruit upon the market at the most suitable and advantageous times and securing better prices.

" There are several ways of attaining this end. In this country we must use some apparatus for the purpose, but in more favoured climes sun drying is still in use ; and even there the system of artificial evaporation, or evaporation by the aid of machinery, is making headway. The same may be said of kiln-dried produce, neither of which will bear comparison with properly evaporated fruit, because they are in an entirely different chemical condition and altogether inferior in quality. Evaporated fruit will keep longer, is less acid, more wholesome, and glucose or fruit sugar is formed and retained, whilst in the old process of slow drying it is entirely lost. All animal and vegetable life is killed by the new process.

" I will now describe the construction of the machine, and, although the greater part consists of wood, there is no danger from fire under ordinary circumstances. First, there is a furnace or stove made of cast iron and standing on iron legs. The stove has corrugated sides enclosed in an iron jacket, which allows the fresh air to enter at the bottom, and passing upwards between the outside jacket and the stove, is thoroughly heated before entering the machine. From the back of the stove proceeds an iron pipe for the purpose of carrying away the smoke produced, and it can be extended any length required to convey the smoke directly outside the building or into any neighbouring flue or chimney. Above this stands an iron chamber in which the different currents of heated air are thoroughly mixed before entering the inclined flue or drying chamber of the evaporator. This chamber may be increased in size with an extra wooden part should the necessity arise for raising the lower end of the evaporator, as in the case of the stove being placed in a low or under-ground position. The evaporator proper consists of a wooden trunk divided into two parts—upper and lower—and rests on the iron air chamber at an angle of about 18°. In this inclined flue consists the superiority over other evaporators.

" The machine is supplied with trays of wooden framework and wire-woven bottoms, on which the articles to be dried are thinly spread. These are entered in tiers of two in the old pattern or deep trays, and in threes in the new pattern or low trays, which are then pushed forward as others are entered until the machine is full.

" The method of preparing the apples to be evaporated is as follows :—They are first pared, cored, and sliced by the Electra, a very simple and ingenious machine which will either pare, core, and slice the apples, or, by removing a knife, will only pare them as for whole apples or the so-called Normandy Pippins. After the apples have been pared, cored, and sliced they are placed in a tub of perfectly clean water, containing a small quantity of salt, which prevents oxidation and discolouration. They are then cut once vertically, and all bruises, specks, and parings trimmed away to produce the well-known apple rings of commerce. They are then placed thinly on a tray and entered at the lower end of the *upper* flue. Sometimes a little sulphur may be sprinkled on the furnace with great advantage for the purpose of bleaching the rings. The first tray remains in the position just mentioned until the second tray is ready—which will be in four or five minutes —to be placed under the first tray ; the third tray is then filled in the usual manner and placed under the second tray, and when the fourth tray is ready the first three trays are pushed forward in the flue, and the fourth tray takes the place of No. 1, and so on until the top flue is full.

"On the arrival of the first tray at the upper end of the flue the contents are examined, and those which are sufficiently dried are removed, and the remainder turned over and returned down the lower and cooler flue. In many cases one tray will hold the whole of the contents (which are nearly dried) of two or three trays, the empty ones being taken away to be again filled with fresh fruit.

"The degree of heat used for drying apples is from 175° to 240° Fahrenheit ; and the time occupied varies from two to four hours, according to the variety of the apple, but from two to two-and-a-half hours is the usual time. Whole apples require a much longer time, eight to ten hours, according to size and variety.

"Plums are dried in the same manner except that they are placed in the evaporator at once. They should be graded according to size and be uniformly ripe. During the process of evaporation plums ought to be removed from the evaporator once or twice for the purpose of cooling them and toughening the skin and so prevent bursting, which they are liable to do because the skin does not allow the moisture in the fruit to freely escape when first placed in the machine. As soon as the plums commence to shrivel all danger of bursting is past, and they may then remain in the evaporator until dry. The time required for plums is from eight to ten hours. Plums may be steamed for a few minutes and then split in half, thus entirely dispensing with the cooling process and considerably reducing the length of time required in drying.

"Apricots are dried in the same manner as plums but without the cooling, and they should be split in halves before being placed in the evaporator.

"Peaches should first be peeled and then treated similarly to apricots.

" Pears ought to be pared, cut in halves, and cored. Small pears may be dried whole after being peeled, no other preparation being necessary, but steaming is sometimes an advantage.

" Cherries require exactly the same treatment as plums but do not take so long to dry.'

" Figs ought to be placed in the evaporator at once and treated the same as plums but without the cooling process.

" Currants of all kinds only require "grading" before being dried. Time, two to three hours.

" French beans and scarlet-runners are sliced in the same manner as when prepared for cooking. Place them in water as they are sliced until there is sufficient to fill a tray, and then put them in the evaporator in a brisk heat and treat in exactly the same manner as for apple rings. Time required about two hours.

" Green peas ought to be treated similarly to French beans (but not sliced ?)

" Asparagus and tomatoes may also be successfully dried.

" Herbs of all kinds are dried with great advantage. They are placed on the trays—not too thickly—and entered in the upper flue. On their arrival at the top or upper end they will be found almost sufficiently dried. Withdraw them and rub them slightly on the trays, and all that is thoroughly dry will then fall through the wire bottoms ; then double the quantity of the remainder which is not sufficiently dry and return it down the lower flue. On its arrival at the bottom all will be thoroughly dry, and only the rough stalks will be left after the final rubbing.

" The evaporator may be used for drying any kind of vegetable, animal, or mineral substance that requires to be preserved in such manner. In India it is used for drying flesh for future use.

" We will now view the question of drying fruit from a commercial point. The cost of labour is not excessive ; one person with a paring and coring machine can dry about 400 pounds of apples, with a No. 2 machine, in a day of twenty-four hours, using an average of seventy-five pounds of coal. A bushel of green apples weighing fifty-six pounds and of medium size will yield about forty-five pounds of "meat" so-called, thus leaving eleven pounds of waste. The forty-five pounds of prepared rings will produce about ten pounds of dried apple rings, different varieties of apples making a little difference in the results as to weight. The dried rings will sell at fourpence to fivepence per pound. The peel and cores are dried and used for the purpose of making apple jelly, consequently the actual waste is reduced to a minimum.

"The best varieties for drying are the good cooking sorts such as Hawthornden, Golden Noble, Dumelow's Seedling, Ecklinville, Warner's King, &c., but any variety may be dried; and, as a rule, the higher the quality of the apple the better will be the quality of the dried article produced. Lemon peel also proves a great success, samples of which have been lately much admired at several important exhibitions.

"In conclusion, it must always prove an advantage to be able to use any kind of fruit in a profitable manner, the owner of which would never find himself in the want of material for the compote or the apple pie, &c., at any season of the year.

"Both the fruit and vegetables require to be soaked some hours in water before use, when they will be found to return to about their normal size and weight, and will be found to retain the juiciness and full flavour of freshly gathered fruit.

"I am convinced that fruit drying would prove a profitable undertaking if worked upon a large scale; and should an evaporator be established in some of our large fruit growing centres, and its usefulness demonstrated to the fruit growing community, it would prove a great benefit both to the growers and the consumers."

After Mr. Trotter's clear exposition of the evaporator, its management and utility, little more can be said with any advantage, and I commend the work of fruit drying to the careful consideration of all who are interested in its culture, and to those who have the general welfare of the community at heart.

CHAPTER XV.

With the hope that my book may have a larger sphere of usefulness I venture to include a few hints upon, and selections of, Window Plants and Hardy Flowers.

WINDOW PLANTS.

FLOWERING PLANTS SUITABLE FOR WINDOWS.

Amaryllis purpurea (Scarboro' Lily)

,, belladonna (Belladonna Lily).

Begonia Weltoniensis

,, nitida

,, insignis

,, maculata

,, parviflora

Campanula isophylla (Bell Flower)

,, pyramidalis (Chimney-pot Flower)

Chrysanthemum Comte de Chambord (Marguerite)

Chrysanthemum Etoile d'Or (Yellow Marguerite)

Crassula coccinea (Kalosanthus)

Calceolarias

Callas (Lily of the Nile)

Coronilla glauca

Phyllocactus Ackermannii (Cactus)

,, Jenkinsonii (,,)

Petunias

Diplacus aurantiacus

Deutzia gracilis

Dielytra spectabilis

Francoa racemosa (Bridal Wreath plant)

Fuchsias

Genista

Heliotrope

Lysimachia nummularia) Money-wort)

Liliums

Mimulus moschœtus (Musk)

Myrtle

Nerium oleander (Oleander)

Pelargoniums, Zonale (Geranium)

,, Variegated (,,)

,, Show (,,

,, Ivy-leaved (,,)

Primula obconica

Saxifraga sarmentosa (Mother-of-Thousands)

There are numerous other plants which will last for a short time in a window, but I prefer to omit all such from my lists and to mention only those plants which will live for years in a window, provided ordinary care is bestowed upon them.

WINDOW PLANTS GROWN ONLY FOR THEIR FOLIAGE.

Aralia Sieboldii
Aspidistra lurida variegata
Acacia lophantha
Bambusa metake (Hardy Bamboo)
Cactus (of sorts)
Carex japonica fol. variegata
Dracœna australis
,,   viridis
Eucalyptus globulus
Ficus elastica (India-rubber) plant
Gasteria
Grevillea robusta
Haworthias
Ornithogalum longibracteatum
(Onion Plant)
Sibthorpia europea
Isolepis gracilis
Aloes, of kinds

PALMS:

Chamærops humilis
,,   excelsa
,,   Fortunei
Livistona australis

FERNS:

Adiantum cuneatum (Maiden-hair)
,,   capillus veneris (Maiden-hair)
Asplenium bulbiferum
,,   marinum (spleenwort)
Athyrium Filix-fœmina (Lady fern)
Cyrtomium falcatum
Davallia canariensis (Hares-foot fern)
Lastrea
Lomaria gibba
Onychium japonicum
Osmunda regalis (Royal fern)
Polypodium vulgare cambricum (Welsh Polybody)
Polystichum angulare proliferum
Pteris serrulata
,,   tremula
Scolopendrium (Harts tongue)

USEFUL HINTS.

Window plants require water, air, light, food and cleanliness. Always saturate the whole mass of soil when water is applied at all.

Let the plants have fresh air, but do not subject them to draughts; a chill is as harmful to them as to yourself.

Give them all the light and sunshine they can bear without apparent injury. Turn the plants round weekly.

Apply food in sufficient quantity to maintain healthy vigour ; a teaspoonful of Clay's or Standen's manure fortnightly during the growing season, or liquid manure " *weak* and *often.*"

Keep the plants as clean as possible, both from insect pests and from accumulations of dust. Those with large leaves and palms may easily be sponged, using soapy water. Strong-growing ferns are benefited by an occasional syringing, also the flowering plants when not in flower. All—except the delicate maidenhair fern—may be exposed to gentle rain in warm weather with great advantage.

Aphis, Red Spider and Thrips may easily be destroyed by placing the infested plants in a small room, shed, large box, or anything which will hold the plants and retain the smoke or vapour, and using carefully an XL All Vaporiser. Scale should be removed by means of a sponge and soapy water, the latter to be at the rate of about two ounces of soft soap, or washing soap, to one gallon of water.

When re-potting a plant be sure that the fresh pot is perfectly clean *inside* as well as outside. Drain the pot well with potsherds, and cover the latter with long moss. Pot firmly, *i.e.*, make the new soil around the plant as solid as the old ball of soil. Let the plant be thoroughly watered several hours before potting.

SOILS FOR—

Flowering Plants, Foliage, Palms — Loam 3 parts, Leaf-mould 1 part, Sand 1 part.

Ferns—
Loam 2 parts,
Leaf-mould 1 part,
Peat & Sand 1 part each.

Cactaceous Plants—

Loam 3 parts,

Old Mortar 1 part,

Sand 1 part,

Dried Cow Manure 1 part.

LIQUID MANURE

may be made from one pound of Guano to twenty gallons of water ; or one peck of soot and one peck of sheep or horse manure to thirty gallons of water ; or one peck of fowl or pigeon manure to thirty gallons of water.

CHAPTER XVI.

FLOWER CULTURE.

FLOWERS TO GROW FOR MARKET.

Anemones (White), Cornflowers, Carnations, Chrysan-
themums (White), Coreopsis, Doronicums, Delphiniums,
Fritillarias, Galega, Gypsophila, Harpalium, Helianthus,
Iris, Lilies (White), Lupins, Monarda, Narcissus, Poppies
(Shirley, Iceland, Welsh), Phlox, Pentstemous, Pinks
(White), Pyrethrums, Mignonette, Roses, Sweet Peas,
Wallflowers, Violets, Rudbeckias, Lilies of the Valley, Globe
Flowers (Trollius), Sweet Sultan.

SELECT HARDY PERENNIALS FOR COTTAGERS AND OTHERS.

*Achillea serrata flore pleno
  (Milfoil)
  ,,   ptarmica   ,,
Alyssum saxatile (Madwort)
*Antirrhinums (Snap Dragon)
*Aquilegia cœrulea (Columbine)
* ,,   chrysantha
* ,,   canadensis
Aubretia Hendersonii
  ,,   purpurea
Anthemis Kelwayii
*Campanula glomerata
* ,,   grandis alba
* ,,   persicifolia alba
* ,,   latifolia

Alstrœmeria aurea
  ,,   psittacina
*Anemone japonica (Wind-flower)
  ,,   ,,   alba
*Aster amellus (Michaelmas
  Daisies)
* ,,   fortunei
* ,,   elegans
* ,,   Nova Belgiæ
Auricula
*Calochortus luteus (Mariposa Lily)
*   ,,   venustus
*Centaurea montana (Centaury)
* ,,   ,,   alba
Coreopsis grandiflora (Tick-seed)

*Chrysanthemum maximum
      ,,   uliginosum
*Delphinium formosum (Larkspur)
*   ,,   Bernice
  Digitalis (Foxgloves)
*Eryngium amethystinum (Sea Holly)
*Gaillardia grandiflora (Blanket Flower)
*Harpalium rigidum
*Helianthus multiflorus (Dwarf Sunflower)
  Helleborus niger major (Christmas Rose)
*Iris germanica (German Iris)
  Lupinus polyphyllus
  Lychnis chalcedonica
*   ,,   dioica fl. pl.
  Monarda didyma
  Narcissus poeticus fl. pl.
*Papaver nudicaule (Iceland Poppy)
*   ,,   bracteatum
*Pinks, white
*Pyrethrums in variety
  Polygonatum multiflorum (Solomon's Seal)
  Rudbeckia Newmannii
  Scilla sibirica (Squill)
  Spirea aruncus (Meadow Sweet
* ,, ulmaria fl. pl.
   ,, filipendua
  Veronicas (Speedwell) of sorts
  Violets

*Carnations
*Clematis erecta
  Dictamnus fraxinella (Fraxinella)
   ,,   ,,   alba
*Doronicum austriacum (Leopard's bane)
*Fritillaria imperialis (Crown Imperial)
*Galega officinalis (Goats Rue)
*Gypsophila paniculata
*Hesperis matronalis fl. pl. (Rocket)
  Helenium pumilum
*Lilium candidum (White Lily)
  Lavatera trinervis
  Mimulus moschata (Musk)
*Meconopsis cambrica (Welsh Poppy)
  Myosotis dissitiflora (Forget-me-not)
  Œnothera Fraseri (Evening Primrose)
  Pentstemons Pœonies
*Phlox decussata varieties
  Polemonium cœruleum (Jacob's Ladder)
   ,,   ,,   album
  Polyanthus and Primroses
  Saxifraga umbrosa (London Pride)
*Solidago altissima (Golden Rod)
   ,, humilis
  Trollius europeus (Globe Flower)
   ,, Fortuneii fl. pl.
  Lily of the Valley (Convallaria)

The 50 genera and species marked with an * are easy to grow, effective in appearance, and are useful for cutting for market purposes or for home decoration. White flowers are in greater demand than coloured flowers. The months of October, November, March and April are the best for planting perennials. Carnations should be layered at the beginning of July, they then quickly root. White Lilies ought to be divided and planted *immediately* after flowering, when division is necessary.

Perennials require sustenance as well as other plants, therefore, place a little manure or decayed leaves about them each autumn, winter, or spring.

Do not disturb the plants too frequently or allow them to be injured by the careless use of the spade or fork about them.

Perennials are plants which live more than two years ; some make growth above ground which dies down again each year like Delphiniums and Phloxes; others do not, like Irises, Carnations, and London Pride.

PERENNIALS FOR SHADY BORDERS.

Anemone japonica, Auriculas, Foxgloves, Iris germanica, Willow Weed (Epilobium), Christmas Roses, London Pride, Solomon's Seal, Phlox suffruticosa, Michaelmas Daisies, Pœonies, Aconites, Squills, Blue Bells, Snowdrops, Primroses, Polyanthus, Golden Rod, Lily of the Valley, Cow Parsnip (Heracleum giganteum), Clematis Jackmannii, Virginian Creeper, Ivy and Ferns.

It must not be understood that the aforementioned plants will succeed better in shade than in sunshine, because they will *not* ; but they are most likely to thrive better under such conditions—and they usually do—than many other plants.

FLOWERS FOR SMOKY DISTRICTS.

Alyssum, Arabis, Anemones, Antirrhinums, Aquilegias, Auriculas (Alpine), Michaelmas Daisies, Carnations, Digitalis, Sunflowers, Iris, Crocus, Oriental Poppy, Pyrethrums, Solomon's Seal, Ænotheras, Golden Rod, London Pride, Jacob's Ladder, Polyanthus, Pœonies, Blue Bells, Candytuft, Sweet Sultan, Mignonette, Mimulus, Silene, Saponaria, Tropæolum, Wallflowers, Honesty, Pinks, Sweet Williams, Stocks, Asters.

CHAPTER XVII.

FLOWER CULTURE.

HARDY ANNUALS FOR FLOWER-BEDS AND FLOWER-BORDERS. SELECTION OF KINDS.

NAME.	Height	Colour.	Time to Sow.	Native Country.
*Bartonia aurea	1½ ft.	Yellow	April 1-15	California
*Calliopsis Burridgei	3 ,,	Crimson and Yell.	,,	Texas
,, bicolor	3 ,,	,, ,		
,, lanceolata	2 ,,	Lemon	,,	,,
*Candytuft, mixed (Iberis)	1 ,,	Various.	Mar. to May	Europe
*Chrysanthemum tricolor	2-3 ,,	White, Yell., Black	April 1-15	,,
,, Burridgeanum	2-3 ,,	White, Yell., Crim.	,,	,,
*Cornflowers (Centaurea)	2-3 ,,	Blue	,,	Britain
*Clarkia of sorts	1½ ,,	Various	,,	North America
Collinsia bicolor	1 ,,	White and Lilac	,,	California
,, grandiflora	1 ,,	White and Purple	,,	Columbia
*Convolvolus major, of sorts	10-14 ,,	Various	, 15-30	
,, minor, ,,	1 ,,		,,	
*Eschscholtzia californica	1 ,,	,,	,, 1-15	California
crocea	1 ,,	Orange and Crim.		

NAME.	Height	Colour.	Time to Sow.	Native Countr
*Delphinium Ajacis (Rocket)	1½ ft.	Various	April 1-15	Tauria
,,　divaricatum (branching)	2½ ,,			Persia
Leptosiphon carmineus	½ ,,	Crimson.	,.	Califorr
Love-lies-bleeding (Amaranthus caudatus)	2 ,,	,,	,, 15-30	Philipp Islan
*Lupinus Hartwegii	2 ,,	Blue and White	,,	Califor
,,　hybridus albo-coccineus	2 ,,	Crimson and White	,,	
Malope grandiflora	2 ,,	Crimson	,,	South Europe
*Godetia Duchess of Albany	1 .,	White	,,	Mexico Chili
*　,,　Lady Albemarle	1 ,,	Crimson		.,
Mignonette (Reseda)	1 ,,	White to Green.	April	Egypt
Mimulus guttatus (Spotted Monkey-flower)	½-1 ,,	Various	,, 15-30	North Americ
*Nemophila insignis	½ ,,	Blue	1-15	Califo
Nigella hispanica (Love-in-a-mist)	¾ ,,	Blue and White		Spain
Œnothera (Evening Primrose)	1-2 ,,	Yellow	,.	North Americ
,,　bistorta Veitchii	1 ,,	Yellow and Crim.		,,
*Phacelia campanularia	1 ,,	Blue	,.	Califor
*Poppy, Shirley	1-2 ,,	Various		Britai hybri
*Salpiglossis, Large-flowering	2 ,,		., 15-30	Chili
*Saponaria calabrica	½ ,,	Pink	,.	Calabr
*　,,　ocymoides	½ ,,	Rose Pink		

NAME.	Height	Colour	Time to Sow.	Native Country.
*Silene pendula compacta	⅓ ft.	Bright Pink	April 15-30	Sicily
flore pleno	¾ ,,	Pink		
*Schizanthus papilionaceus	2 ,,	Various		Chili
* ,, pinnatus roseus	2 ,,	Rose	,,	,,
*Sweet Peas(Pisum elatum)	6 ,,	Various	March	Iberia
*Sweet Sultan (Centaurea)	1½ ,,	Various	April	Persia
Tropœolum majus (Nasturtium)	6-10,,	Crimson and Yell.		Peru
,, peregrinum (canary creeper)	6-10 ,,	Yellow	,.	Peru and Mexico
Virginian Stock (Malcomia)	½ ,,	Various	,,	Europe
Viscaria cardinalis	1½ ,,	Majenta	,,	Algiers
,, elegans picta	1½ ,,	Crim. and White		
, oculata	1½ ,,	Pink, dark eye		

Of the foregoing 31 genera those marked * will probably give most satisfaction.

" Annuals " are plants which grow from seed, flower, and die in one year under ordinary conditions of their requirements of growth.

These plants require good soil and space for developement if the best results are to be attained. Thin them freely when the seedlings are large enough to handle ; those a foot and more in height ought to be left from six inches to a foot apart, with the exception of Sweet Peas ; those less than a foot in height should be left from three to six inches apart.

Packets of seed may be purchased at prices varying from one penny to one shilling each, in quantities to suit all gardens. A good display of hardy annuals may be produced for the first cost of half-a-crown.

Very small seeds ought to be only just covered with soil; those a little larger may be sown half-an-inch deep; and one inch is deep enough for the largest seeds, except Peas and Lupins, which require to be sown about two inches deep.

HARDY BIENNIALS.

Plants which grow from seed one year, and flower, seed, and die the second year under ordinary conditions of growth.

NAME.	Height	Colour.	Times to Sow.	Plant out permanentl
Campanula calycanthema	2½ ft.	Blue	April	October
,, ,, alba	,,	White	..	
,, media (Canterbury bells)	,,	Various		
Wallflowers (Cheiranthus Cheirii)	1½ ,,	Crimson, Yellow		Sept. & Oc·
,, double German	,,	Various		
Honesty (Lunaria biennis)	2½ ,,	Purple and White	,,	
Indian Pinks (Dianthus Heddewigii)	1 ,,	Various	April & May	
Sweet Williams (Dianthus barbatus)	1 ,,			
Brompton Stocks (Mathiola simplicicaulis)	2 ,,	Scarlet, White	May or June	

Hardy Annuals and Biennials are plants which do not require shelter or protection from an ordinary amount of frost when under average cultural conditions.

Tender Annuals are well known in Asters, Ten-week Stocks, Zinnias, Helichrysums, and Phlox Drummondii.

Tender Biennials are of no real value to the small gardener, though no well-managed flower-garden would be complete without some representatives.

Mark & Moody's Publications.

NEW PICTURES IN OLD FRAMES, being a book of verse for Girls and Boys, written in old French forms by Gertrude Bradley & Amy Mark. Pictured by G.B., lettered by A.M., written by them both ; 3s. 6d.

THE STEWPONEY FARMERS' ACCOUNT BOOK. Adapted for one year or longer if required. Foolscap folio, half-bound, 6s.

CLENTINE RAMBLES. A guide to Hagley and Clent. Foolscap 8vo., 1s. ; or with a List of Flowering Plants of the District, 2s.

PENNY GUIDE TO HAGLEY AND CLENT. Demy 8vo., with Illustrations and Map (per post 2d).

HEATING BY HOT WATER. By Walter Jones ; a complete treatise on high and low pressure heating, with numerous illustrations. Crown 8vo., cloth gilt, 2s. 6d.

THE LYTTELTON CRICKET SCORING BOOK. Books, 3d., 6d., 1s., 3s. 6d., and 6s. each. Sheets, 1d. each.

CRAUFURD'S SERMONS. I, on his Second Marriage ; II, A Few Words on Ditto ; III, " How about a Day of Humiliation ? " Demy 8vo., 6d. each.

THE CHRIST OF GOD. Expository Notes, by J. Dingley. Demy 8vo., 48 p.p., 9d.

JOHN CORBETT, Esq., OF IMPNEY. A Sketch with Portrait and Views. Crown 8vo., 24 p.p., 6d. ; cloth gilt, 1s.

STOURBRIDGE ALMANACK & DIRECTORY. Demy 8vo., 70 p.p., 3d.

STOURBRIDGE   MARK & MOODY.

PRINTING.

The attention of the public is called to the complete Printing Plant of the " County Express " Offices. The following Branches are worked on the premises :—

LETTER-PRESS

LITHOGRAPHIC, Coloured and Plain.

COPPER-PLATE

STEREOTYPING

Large and Powerful Machines for big Posting Bills.

Fast Cylinder Machines for small cheap work in large quantities.

Special Machines for the highest-class Bookwork and Artistic Printing.

ESTIMATES FREE.

MARK & MOODY,

STOURBRIDGE.

TELEPHONE No. 8516.

The 'County Express'

For Worcestershire and Staffordshire.

Saturdays, 1d.   Established 1867.

The leading Newspaper for Mid and North Worcestershire and South Staffordshire, having a wide circulation throughout these Mining, Manufacturing, Agricultural and Residential Districts.

Full Local Reports,

Athletic News,

Chess Column,

(Conducted by Mr. BELLINGHAM.

CHARGES FOR CHEAP PREPAID ADVERTISEMENTS.

Not exceeding	1 Inser.		3 Inser.		6 Inser.	
24 words	1	0	2	0	3	0
32 ,,		3	2	6	3	9
40		6	3	0	4	6
48 ,,	1	9	3	6	5	3
56 ,,	2	0	4	0	6	0

Special Terms for advertisements for 3, 6, and 12 months.

OFFICES :—

STOURBRIDGE (Head Office)	135, High Street
KIDDERMINSTER	23, High Street.
DUDLEY	70, High Street.
BRIERLEY HILL	49, High Street.
CRADLEY HEATH	81, High Street.

BIRMINGHAM AGENT, Mr. Fred Mundy, 26, Temple Street.

Telephone No. 8516.

CPSIA information can be obtained at www.ICGtesting.com
Printed in the USA
BVOW06s0852120816

458761BV00021B/138/P